Paradoxical
Thinking

Paradoxical Thinking

Thinking

How to Profit from
Your Contradictions

JERRY FLETCHER / KELLE OLWYLER

Berrett-Koehler Publishers, Inc.
San Francisco

Berrett-Koehler Publishers, Inc.
450 Sansome Street, Suite 1200
San Francisco, CA 94111-3320
Tel: (415) 288-0260 Fax: (415) 362-2512

Ordering Information

Individual sales. Berrett-Koehler publications are available through most bookstores. They can also be ordered direct from Berrett-Koehler at the address above.

Quantity sales. Special discounts are available on quantity purchases by corporations, associations, and others. For details, contact the "Special Sales Department" at the Berrett-Koehler address above.

Orders for college textbook/course adoption use. Please contact Berrett-Koehler Publishers at the address above.

Orders by U.S. trade bookstores and wholesalers. Please contact Publishers Group West, 4065 Hollis Street, Box 8843, Emeryville, CA 94662. Tel: (510) 658-3453; 1-800-788-3123. Fax: (510) 658-1834

Printed in the United States of America

 Printed on acid-free and recycled paper that is composed of 50% recovered fiber, including 10% postconsumer waste.

Library of Congress Cataloging-in-Publication Data

Fletcher, Jerry, 1941–
    Paradoxical thinking: how to profit from your contradictions /
Jerry Fletcher. Kelle Olwyler. — 1st ed.
      p. cm.
    ISBN 1-881052-80-x (alk. paper)
    1. Success in business. 2. Paradox. 3. Conduct of life.
I. Olwyler, Kelle, 1950– . II. Title.
HF5386.F418   1997
650.1—dc21   97-16704
                                 CIP

First Edition
00 99 98 97   10 9 8 7 6 5 4 3 2 1

Copyediting and proofreading: PeopleSpeak
Interior design and production: Joel Friedlander Publishing Services
Pendulum drawing: Martha Weston
Indexing: Rachel Rice
Cover: Cassandra Chu

Dedication

For Kathleen and Max, our respective spouses, who have patiently provided us with honest feedback, yet unmitigated support, throughout the writing of this book. And for Jerry's eleven-year-old daughter, Cassie, whose directness, honesty, and zestful approach to life has continually reminded us of what we hope the tools in this book will help adults bring back into their lives.

Contents

Preface

Paradoxical Thinking is a practice that we use every day in our own lives and have taught for more than a decade. Nearly everyone has found it practical, powerful, and profitable.

We particularly value the Paradoxical Thinking tools, and we believe you will too, because they can be used by ordinary people to improve their performance in their jobs and in their lives. More often than you probably think is possible, you will be able to bring together two seemingly disparate ideas and capabilities into a fresh new approach to accomplishing something that had stymied your best thinking.

Our original interest in paradox came from very different directions: Jerry from his observation that very successful people seem almost universally to be contradictory and apparently more "comfortable" with their contradictions than the rest of us; Kelle from a truly cross-cultural upbringing (her American parents raised her in a Latin culture) in which she constantly had to deal with contradictory expectations. We began working together in 1986 because of our mutual commitment to giving people practical tools with which they can improve their ability to meet their life's goals, whatever they may be.

The Association of High Performance and Paradox

This book grew out of our experiences in enabling people to achieve and sustain levels of high performance way beyond their expectations. In a previous book, *Patterns of High Performance: Discovering the Ways People Work Best,* Jerry defined "high performance" as "the experience of having an activity 'take off' and go much better than expected" (for example, a meeting with a customer that ended up with a sale twice as big as expected; a speech that moved an audience to tears or uproarious laughter; a golf game that included a string of pars). For that book, he collected thousands of detailed stories about how individuals achieve high levels of performance. Through a detailed analysis of these stories, he identified what he calls a "High Performance Pattern," a description of the process each person uses to succeed.

Our detailed analysis of many thousands of these individual high performance episodes alerted us to the unique way people use paradoxical qualities in creating success. We discovered that *individuals are always paradoxical when they are performing at their best.* More importantly, each individual seems to express a particular and unique paradox when achieving his or her best results.

Paradoxical Thinking Works

We began to teach people to find the unique combination of their paradoxical qualities that leads to their success. We developed simple tools to help them use these qualities deliberately in dealing with problems and opportunities. We found, to the delight of people with whom we came into contact, that the insights provided by these tools enabled our clients to make significant progress on problems that had been stymieing them, sometimes for years. We could enable clients to achieve much better and more satisfying results by taking an openly paradoxical approach.

As we validated this idea with more and more individuals, we began to see how the conventional wisdom that human beings ought to be consistent to be effective might be wrong, at least in many circumstances. Indeed, a far more powerful approach to improving performance seems to be to understand the nature of your paradoxical qualities, learn which ones work together to produce outstanding results, and then learn how to put those qualities into action.

Paradoxical Thinking also works with teams and organizations to help them expand their ideas, become high performing, and sustain a new level of success. The extension of the process to groups requires a few adjustments, which we describe in Chapter 12, but the payoff is at least as powerful.

Paradoxical Thinking is a way of intentionally searching for the potential in people and situations and celebrating that potential. It is a way of thinking that supports our deeply held belief that every individual has unique, inherent strengths and talents that can be cultivated to produce ingenious, highly effective, and extremely satisfying results.

We believe this process generates core insights and fresh ways of understanding that lead to more rewarding actions and interactions. When taken with enthusiasm and confidence, these actions unleash elevated and sustainable levels of human performance. As we have directly experienced, once people are exposed to this kind of thinking, they *expand their valuing of themselves* as well as of those with whom they interact in their everyday lives.

Conversely, we find appalling the amount of wasted time and effort that human beings spend in frustrating cycles of ineffectiveness: trying over and over again to make something work with their usual combination of intelligence and effort. After awhile, even the most confident feel powerless and angry and lose their belief in their own capabilities. If this book can help people think and act more creatively, using their paradoxical qualities consciously, to make something positive happen, we will be delighted.

Throughout our own exploration of paradox and how it works, we continually learn and expand our own thinking. We have been elated and at times deeply humbled by the truly awesome nature of human beings functioning at their best. We offer our insights and present examples to help you begin your own exploration in the art of Paradoxical Thinking.

Acknowledgments

While we have written this book and are the developers of the tools described here, it is also true that virtually every associate of High Performance Dynamics has contributed. We would particularly like to mention Edward Hinkelman, Dee Thompson, Geri Blitzman, Terry Pearce, Richard Snyder, Meryem LeSaget, Philip Collings, and a myriad of others who in the process of learning the Paradoxical Thinking process and then using it with clients, taught us more about it. We also would like to thank the wonderfully patient staff of our publisher, Berrett-Koehler. With Jerry's first book, he had an advanced draft before they agreed to publish it. Thus he was able to meet all of the deadlines easily. With this one, they undoubtedly expected the same ease of production. We, on the other hand, greatly underestimated how difficult it would be to make our experience work as a book. As we kept extending our deadline, the

Berrett-Koehler staff managed to be consistently supportive. We greatly appreciate their encouragement and their belief that this book was worth waiting for.

Jerry L. Fletcher   Kelle Olwyler

San Anselmo, CA   Novato, CA

April 1997   April 1997

What Is Paradoxical Thinking

Paradoxical Thinking is an active process. Once you learn it, you can use it to keep yourself on course, even when you are in the middle of difficult, fast-changing situations. However, to teach it, we have slowed it down to provide you with detailed information about the process.

Thus, the first six chapters provide an introduction to the concept of Paradoxical Thinking (chapter 1) and as detailed a description of each step as we have been able to create (chapters 2–6). To illustrate each of the five steps, we follow two people all the way through the process and describe how they apply the steps to improve their results in difficult situations.

Here is a brief summary of what is in each chapter:

» Chapter 1, "Effective Paradoxes" provides some definitions, a little theory and a number of examples and introduces the two people we use to illustrate the steps in the process.

» Chapter 2, "Finding Your Core Personal Paradox" helps you find a key pair of personal paradoxical characteristics you can use to achieve more positive results in difficult situations.

» Chapter 3, "Perception-Shifting" shows you how to see the positive value of what you may have always assumed was a negative trait and see the negatives in what you always assumed was a positive trait. The result is a much more expanded view of your capabilities.

» Chapter 4, "Defining Your Problem Situation and Setting Your Goal" provides a simple way to define the results you want in a difficult situation so that Paradoxical Thinking can help you see a fresh way to achieve your goal.

» Chapter 5, "Rating Yourself on Fletcher's Pendulum" describes a simple way of assessing how well your actions are working to improve the difficult situation you are in.

» Chapter 6, "Choosing Action Steps to Improve Your Self-Ratings" provides guidelines for setting up an action plan to improve your performance.

Paradoxical Thinking at a Glance

Below is a quick overview of the steps of the Paradoxical Thinking process. These steps will mean much more after you have read the chapters, and then this list will be a convenient summary reference.

1. *Finding Your Core Personal Paradox.* Identifying contradictory aspects of yourself and selecting one that represents a core tension with which you struggle.

   1a. List your personal qualities and characteristics

   1b. Combine these personal qualities and characteristics into paradoxical pairs using oxymorons

   1c. Select one combination that describes a central conflict or tension you struggle with

2. *Perception-Shifting.* Breaking open your narrow judgments about the positive or negative value of your contradictory qualities. Then identifying the high performance and nightmare expressions of your core personal paradox.

   2a. List positives of preferred side
   List the positive expressions of the side of your core personal paradox—your oxymoron—that you like best.

   2b. List negatives of preferred side
   List the negative (extreme) expressions of the side of your core personal paradox that you like best.

   2c. List negatives of disliked side
   List the negative (extreme) expressions of the side of your core personal paradox—your oxymoron—that you like least.

   2d. List positives of disliked side
   List the positive expressions of the side of your core personal paradox that you like least.

   2e. Choose a High Performance Oxymoron
   Choose a "High Performance Oxymoron" for yourself that captures the positive expression of both sides of your core personal paradox.

   2f. Choose a Nightmare Oxymoron
   Choose a "Nightmare Oxymoron" for yourself that captures the negative expression of both sides of your core personal paradox.

3. *Defining Your Problem Situation and Setting Your Goal.* Picking an important, current problem that is not going as well as you would like and defining it so that you can use Paradoxical Thinking on it.

3a. Describe your unsatisfactory choices
Describe the problem situation in terms of its unsatisfactory choices, as you currently see them.

3b. Explain the situation's effects on you
Explain how this problem situation affects you personally.

3c. Assess your past efforts
Describe what you have tried so far and what happened.

3d. Write a goal statement with a deadline
Write a complete, measurable goal statement, with a deadline.

4. *Rating Yourself on Fletcher's Pendulum.* Deciding for yourself how well you are expressing both sides of your high performance paradox with respect to this problem or goal.

4a. Set up your own personal pendulum

4b. Place your goal at the top

4c. Define the expression of each side
Define how you would be acting toward your goal if you were expressing the high performance and nightmare of one side of your oxymoron.
Then define how you would be acting toward your goal if you were expressing the high performance and nightmare of the other side of your oxymoron.

4d. Rate your current actions with respect to your goal

5. *Choosing Action Steps to Improve Your Self-Ratings.* Identifying action steps you are willing to take to more fully express your paradoxical qualities with respect to this problem or goal.

5a. List action steps you will take to raise your self-ratings of your lower side

5b. List action steps you will take to raise your self-ratings of your higher side

1

Effective Paradoxes

We have to find ways to make sense of . . . paradoxes, to use them to shape a better destiny.

—CHARLES HANDY
The Age of Paradox

You can probably remember times in your life when you faced a really daunting task and handled it with great focus, internal calm, and centeredness despite its difficulty. It may have been

» Taking on a volatile situation involving angry and disgruntled employees and successfully turning their attitudes around.

» Confronting an employee accused of sexual harassment or alcoholism who denied it all, and after a careful investigation, successfully getting him to acknowledge the problem and seek help.

» Convincing a competitor's biggest customer to switch to your product.

» Holding your own against a far more experienced negotiator to achieve a difficult agreement.

» Meeting with upset financial analysts when your company was in serious trouble and handling every question so thoroughly that there was no significant negative publicity.

» Taking a risk to do something you had always wanted to try, but no one ever thought you would, such as bungee jumping, sky diving, or running for political office. And possibly doing it despite vehement opposition from people who knew you.

» Confronting a teenager who was in serious trouble and helping her find a way to make more positive choices.

» Ending a relationship that was going nowhere, despite all your efforts, all the potential, and all the love that existed.

If you are like most people, you have had experiences like these. Afterward you wondered how you managed to stay so focused and centered through it all. You wish you could understand how to prepare yourself for similar future situations so you could face them with the same calm and focus.

You particularly would like to understand the process because you also can remember times when a situation didn't go well at all, for example:

» Losing the account of a valued customer to a clever competitor who outmaneuvered you.

» Letting your opponents provoke you with their questions at a public meeting. You ended up in angry recriminations and finger-pointing, and the issue you cared about so fervently ended up in a protracted court battle that enriched no one but the lawyers.

» Having your boss refuse to give you the raise or the promotion you deserved and leaving his office bitter and resentful.

» Trying to talk to your teenager and ending up in a screaming match for the twenty-fifth time.

What was the difference? What was responsible for your seeming invincibility in some circumstances and your volatility and reactiveness in others? While the details of each incident are very different, we have come to believe there is a common underlying process that accounts for the positive outcomes. If you can learn what that process is for you, you can much more successfully face new and difficult situations.

This core process is difficult to grasp: it has to do with paradox.

What Is Paradox

Webster's Dictionary defines paradox as:

> A statement or proposition seemingly self-contradictory or absurd, and yet explicable as expressing a truth.

More loosely, one of its secondary definitions of paradox is:

> Any person, thing, or act exhibiting apparent contradictions or inconsistencies.

In *Paradox and Transformation: Toward a Theory of Change in Organization and Management*, one of the leading books in the field, Quinn and Cameron define paradox by saying:

> Fundamentally, paradox embraces clashing ideas. Paradox . . . involves contradictory, mutually exclusive elements that are present and operate equally at the same time.

While purists may use the term to refer only to truly mutually exclusive combinations, we use the term "paradox" somewhat more loosely to mean contradictory or *seemingly* impossible combinations of ideas or actions. We prefer the looser definition, for while some paradoxical combination of ideas or actions may seem impossible, often in reality it is not. The seeming impossibility has to do with a person's own limited frame of reference. When a way is found to make both concepts real simultaneously, a deeper truth is revealed. As this book will show, acting in paradoxical, seemingly contradictory ways can produce a creative resolution of a dilemma that had previously proved intractable.

Your Unique Personal Paradox

That individuals have paradoxical qualities has been noted in very nearly every culture. *That individuals can use them to guide their own behavior and profit from their success has not.* Yet understanding how to use your own paradoxical qualities as a tool can enable you to cut through complex, confusing problems and find more effective routes for getting things accomplished.

Not just any paradoxical behavior will improve performance. Rather, each person has a particular combination of contradictory and paradoxical qualities that seem to work together to produce a person's best work. The tools described in subsequent chapters will enable you to find your unique, personal paradox and to consciously use it to improve your capacity for sustained high performance.

Some Provocative Examples

We have found over the years that providing examples helps people understand what we are describing. These examples are not from people with whom we have worked. They do, however, prepare the mind for working with paradox.

Physical Capabilities: Olympic Sprinters

During the trials for the 1996 U.S. Olympic team, Michael Johnson, the great 200 and 400 meter dash competitor, talked about the paradox of running the 400 meters at world record pace. As he put it, "There are a lot of things you have to concentrate on in the 400, and two of them are opposites: aggression and relaxation." He spoke of the one slight mistake he made in eight trial races in Atlanta, where he went "right to the relaxing before the aggressing."[1] He won, but it cost him a world record. Michael went on not only to win gold medals in both the 400 meters and the 200 meters in Atlanta, but also he set a world record in the 200 that obliterated his previous record by 0.35 of a second—a margin of victory that is astonishing at the Olympic level of competition.

During the trials for the 1984 Olympic team, *Sports Illustrated* reported a conversation with the coach of Carl Lewis, the great U.S. sprinter and long jumper. As he was getting ready for a sprint final, Carl's coach was asked if Carl could be beaten. The coach replied that the only way Carl could be beaten was if he pressed coming out of the blocks. So long as he stayed relaxed and trusted that the speed would be there, no one could touch him."[2] Carl went on to win four gold medals. In Atlanta, twelve years later in his fourth Olympics, Carl won yet another gold medal, this one in the long jump.

Most people might assume that sprinters need only to run as hard as they can to win. That is only half the story. Sprinters actually run faster if they can remain relaxed while sprinting. It is when an athlete tightens up in the middle of an event that performance deteriorates. In order to do their best, sprinters need to develop an ability to simultaneously engage the exact opposite quality of what their sport seems to demand: calmness and relaxation.

Paradox, Not Compromise Note that this is not a compromise. Sprinters are not half-relaxed and half-sprinting. This is not a "balance" between relaxation and sprinting. Rather, it is a state of running as hard as they can *and* feeling relaxed, effortless, and flowing while they do.

Sprinting is an example of an activity where sustained high performance requires simultaneously employing what is usually associated with the activity and its opposite. For people who personally are not familiar with the physical experience of simultaneous action and relaxation, it is difficult to provide other analogies, but here are two:

» Eyesight: We have two eyes. Yet when we see, we don't experience two different versions of the same scene. We experience one. Combined, the two different images produce depth, a more powerful result than either eye can give separately.

» Music: There is a form of music called "counterpoint," in which two (or more) different melodies are sung or played by two different musicians at the same time (instead of one melody and one or more harmony parts). The two melodies blend into a combined sound that goes beyond either one separately. Renaissance music commonly incorporated this technique. A close example that most people have experienced is singing a "round," in which the same melody is sung by several groups that begin singing at different times. The combined sound is something quite different from just the melody.

The power of eyesight or counterpoint music comes from the fact that each part holds its own. It has been our finding that at very high levels of performance, apparently paradoxical actions seem to be present simultaneously. But the result is not a compromise as the apparent contradiction would seem to require. Both actions are present fully.

The Creative Process

The creative process advances through the use of opposites. Albert Rothenberg has reviewed the creative processes of a large number of extraordinarily successful writers, poets, and scientists. He has found that central to most creative work is what he calls Janusian Thinking: the ability to conceive of two or more opposites existing simultaneously. He cites, for example, the mental image that a person falling from the roof of a house is both in motion with respect to the ground and at rest with respect to any other objects falling with him. He credits images such as this as the basis of Einstein's Theory of Relativity.[3]

Famous, Successful People

While a number of studies have attempted to identify commonalities among famous, successful people, the paradoxical and contradictory nature of success has for the most part escaped attention. Pick any biography you wish and inevitably, you'll find a section about the often astonishing contradictions of the person's life. Many times the biographer doesn't know what to make of the contradictions, and there is often an implied judgment that there is something wrong with the person because of them.

Yet if the idea is accepted that highly successful people are paradoxical and contradictory, we can ask what that means for the rest of us. Our contention is that particular paradoxes and apparent contradictions are *responsible* for the success of certain people. Here are a few examples.

Bill Gates Microsoft Chairman Bill Gates, about whom volumes have been written, is a bundle of contradictions, many of which are noticed daily by people with whom he interacts. Charming and capable of huge fits of anger, humble and arrogant, Bill Gates doesn't make any pretense of being "consistent" in any narrow sense of that word. One paradox, however, is particularly telling. Stewart Alsop II, the editor of *PC Letter*, describes Bill as a "practical visionary." As Stewart puts it, "He is able to see in his mind's eye where all the technology is leading, but he also knows how to . . . make it happen."[4]

But Alsop's explanation is weaker than Gates deserves. He truly is a remarkable visionary, able for more than a decade now to not only see where technology is heading but also to see the kinds of products and product shifts that are necessary to keep riding the leading edge of the technology wave. Despite the huge size and installed base (existing customer base) of Microsoft, he is also able to recognize mistakes and force abrupt changes, as he did recently when he realized he had missed the importance of the Internet.

On the practical side, he is also remarkable. Even though he hires the smartest programmers and technologists he can find, many of those in the company say he is at least as good as they are with the nuts and bolts technological details. Similar comments have been made by executives at senior levels with respect to his command of, for example, the financial details of the company.

These two traits aren't usually found together. Typically a person who is truly outstanding as a visionary is not able to stay on top of, let alone manage and lead, the practical process of reaching the vision. The broad-scope thinking and the associative, nonlinear thinking characteristic of visionary breakthroughs *interferes with* practical, linear attention to deadline-driven details. Similarly, people who are truly outstanding at the practical details of implementing a vision are rarely good at developing it. Getting mired in the practical details, as well as the linear thinking and goal/deadline-driven process of implementing a vision *interferes with* visionary thinking. Bill Gates manages to do both well simultaneously and has for a long time. What he has is a great combination of capabilities. In most people, these capabilities are paradoxical and mutually exclusive. In him they coexist in a way that is ultimately complementary.

The idea that this paradox is responsible for Gates's success may seem a bit far-fetched to some people. You might be saying to yourself, if he concentrated on one trait or the other, he would be even more effective. We think not.

Consider what would happen if Bill Gates didn't have both strengths. If he just focused on being a visionary, sensing where technology is leading but unable to guide Microsoft to get products into the marketplace in a timely manner, Microsoft soon would not be the number one player in the industry. Similarly, if he only focused on creating and getting practical products out to market, he might miss a key shift in the direction of the technology's development, and other companies could seize the lead.

Numerous other computer companies made such mistakes. The Xerox Research Center actually invented what became the Apple computer interface, but it took Steve Jobs to bring it to market. Word-star once had a lock on word processing, but it failed to get an updated product on the market in time. Wang literally owned the office automation/word processing market and failed to anticipate changes in the direction of technologies.

Charlotte Beers Charlotte Beers is chairman and CEO of Ogilvy & Mather, one of the world's largest advertising agencies. In an interview by Sarah Mahoney in *Town & Country Monthly*, Mahoney described Beers as having a "let's get down to business demeanor tempered by a warm laugh."[5] In a *Fortune* magazine article, two top female executive friends of Beers's, Martha Stewart and Darla Moore, described her as "tenacious and evocative."[6] In a companion *Fortune* article, Patricia Sellers said of Beers, "She is intimate, incisive, tough, and funny." In her own words, Beers says, "I'm likely to say the most outrageous thing in the room—to liven things up."[7]

These traits—very tough and incisive, yet very funny, evocative, and even outrageous—again combine to be much more powerful than any by itself. If she was just tough and incisive, she wouldn't distinguish herself from others in the advertising world, particularly men. If she was just funny and outrageous, she might not be taken seriously. It's the apparently paradoxical combination—a first-class mind and executive toughness combined with outrageous theatricality and warm humor—that make her so effective.

Sam Walton Sam Walton, founder and chairman of Wal-Mart until his death in 1992, wrote an autobiography, *Sam Walton: Made in America, My Story*. It provides not just Sam's version of events, but commentaries on these events and on Sam by a wide variety of people who worked with him. Through anecdote after anecdote a portrait emerges of a man who embodied at least three paradoxes: First, he was relentlessly focused on winning—and he was totally flexible, willing to try anything and to drop whatever didn't work without a second thought. Second, he was ingeniously creative—and willing to copy anything that had worked for someone else. Third, he was one of the best motivators who ever lived, willing to give everyone room to try whatever they thought would work—and somebody who checked up on everything anyone did.[8]

For example, David Glass, CEO of Wal-Mart, described Sam in these paradoxical ways:

> When Sam feels a certain way, he is relentless . . . He will bring up an idea, we'll all discuss it and then decide . . . that maybe it's not something we should be doing right now—or ever. Fine. Case closed. But as long as he thinks it is the right thing, it just keeps coming up— week after week after week—until finally everybody capitulates . . . I guess it could be called management by wearing you down.[9]

and:

> Sam Walton . . . is less afraid of being wrong than anyone I've ever known. And once he sees he's wrong, he just shakes it off and heads in another direction.[10]

His son, Jim Walton, described his father:

> Dad always said you've got to stay flexible. We never went on a family trip, nor have we ever heard of a business trip in which the schedule wasn't changed at least once after the trip was underway.[11]

Or as A. L. Johnson, vice chairman of Wal-Mart, described him:

> As famous as Sam is for being a great motivator—and he deserves even more credit than he's gotten for that—he is equally good at checking on the people he has motivated. You might call his style: management by looking over your shoulder.[12]

These combinations, again, are much more powerful than any one by itself. If all Sam had was a relentless drive to do things his way, he could well have made the common entrepreneurial mistake of sticking with an idea he thought was good long after it wasn't working. If all he had was flexibility, he would have been too apt to change directions before a good idea had time to work. If all he did was motivate people and let them go, they'd be apt to scatter in a thousand directions. If all he did was look over their shoulders and double-check everything they did, action would have slowed to a crawl, and he wouldn't have been able to attract good people. The combination of his paradoxical traits made him unbeatable.

Ken Olsen Ken Olsen, founder and long-time chairman of Digital Equipment Corporation, was described by his biographers:

He manages to be simultaneously flexible and unwavering—flexible in the smaller arenas of decision-making, unwavering in setting direction, policy, and tradition. He is the democrat who has given up great personal control of this sprawling organization of 120,000 employees. But he is also the autocrat who has maintained his power as the final word and has never named a clear second-in-command.[13]

For a very long time—from Digital's founding in the mid-sixties through the late eighties—these paradoxical traits served Olsen and his corporation very well. The combination of control and democracy built a very powerful organization.

We frankly believe this list could be expanded to include any successful executive, or anyone who is successful. People who are effective embody paradoxes.

We now cite two examples from politics.

Bill Clinton A review of a recent book, *First in His Class: A Biography of Bill Clinton* by David Maraniss, includes this statement: "With equal matter-of-fact fascination [Mr. Maraniss] describes his subject's sincerity and calculation, his boldness and cowardice, his calm and his temper tantrums, his loyalty and his infidelities."[14]

In the book itself, Mr. Maraniss writes:

> It is often tempting, but usually misleading, to try to separate the good from the bad, to say that the part of him that is indecisive, too eager to please and prone to deception, is more revealing of the inner man than the part of him that is indefatigable, intelligent, empathetic, and self-deprecating. They co-exist.[15]

Though it is a difficult mental leap, consider that a person can be sincere and calculating at the same time, without either side being false. The willingness to be fully both at the same time may well play a pivotal role in President Clinton's success.

Mario Cuomo In a cover story on Mario Cuomo, who was then governor of New York, about his possible run for president, *Time* magazine opened its article in this way:

> The face, broad and fleshy, with dark-ringed eyes and a gap-toothed smile; the body, stocky and powerful, . . . and the hands, strong and blunt like small shovels—all combine to give him the look of one of the proud immigrants who toiled . . . to build the Brooklyn Bridge.

A laborer, a man capable of bearing heavy weights, a man of explosive passions and simple pleasures. Someone strong. Someone you do not want to tangle with.

Then a rustle of papers, and the man puts on a delicate pair of wire-rim glasses. He begins to talk, to speak in smooth, connected sentences. As if by a conjurer's trick, the laborer is transformed into the scholar, a solitary thinker who shies away from the world of action, a man of introspection who rises early to wrestle with questions of motivation and desire . . .

Mario Matthew Cuomo, the Governor of New York, *is both of these men, the man of strenuous action and the man of otherworldly contemplation.* (Emphasis added)[16]

As this quote makes clear, Cuomo is passionate, strong, and action-oriented, while at the same time intellectual, ascetic, and reflective. It is a mistake to think of him as solely one type of man or the other or to assume that one of his sides is merely a deliberately created political image.

To understand how his two sides together make Cuomo much more formidable than either one separately, look at what would happen if he was just one way or the other. If he was only a passionate, explosive, action-oriented man, without the intellect, he would lack the ability to see through the plethora of demands from contending interest groups to develop a policy that could gain majority support. Conversely, if he was just an intellectual without a passion for action, he would be ineffective at implementing his great ideas. Cuomo's two sides combine to make him someone capable of winning the New York governorship for three four-year terms.

We could cite numerous other examples, but the idea was simply to present in a provocative way the idea that paradoxical capabilities appear to be present simultaneously when people produce outstanding results.

Paradoxical Thinking

We have coined the phrase "Paradoxical Thinking" to describe the process of bringing together consciously the two paradoxical sides of yourself to achieve outstanding results. The process involves five steps:

1. Finding Your Core Personal Paradox. Identifying contradictory aspects of yourself and selecting one that represents a core tension with which you struggle.

2. Perception-Shifting. Breaking open your narrow judgments about the positive or negative value of your contradictory qualities and identifying the high performance expression of your core personal paradox.

3. Defining Your Problem Situation and Setting Your Goal. Picking an important, current problem (relationship, situation) that is not going as well as you would like and defining it so that you can approach it paradoxically.

4. Rating Yourself on Fletcher's Pendulum. Deciding for yourself how well you are expressing both sides of your high performance paradox with respect to a problem or goal.

5. Choosing Action Steps to Improve Your Self-Ratings. Identifying and carrying out action steps to more fully express your paradoxical qualities with respect to this problem or goal.

By following these five steps, you can profit from your contradictions. You can accomplish important and meaningful goals more easily and achieve more powerful results, particularly in the face of previously intractable problems. *The route to sustaining high performance is to consciously and actively encourage yourself to be paradoxical.*

Actually achieving this state is discomforting and challenging because it initially seems illogical and contrary to common sense. However, it is necessary. Creating seamless combinations of usually paradoxical capabilities without compromise can be the route to achieving and sustaining high levels of performance.

Negative Attitudes Toward Paradox

Broadly speaking, American culture finds the notion of paradox difficult to handle. People who believe or hold one position on a controversial issue and act in a way contrary to it are called inconsistent, or worse, hypocritical. A person with distinctly different behavior patterns is referred to routinely (if not diagnosed) as schizophrenic.

While we don't want to minimize the destructive effects of truly psychotic behavior, one of the effects of Americans' attitude toward inconsistent and paradoxical behavior is that all such behavior is regarded as bad. Most people believe that human beings have to be consistent to be effective, and inconsistencies or paradoxes are part of a drift toward pathology. Many psychologists, therapists, counselors, and advisors (not to mention reporters, biographers, and political strategists) operate with an assumption that inconsistencies in human behavior ought to be eliminated.

Destructive Forms of Paradoxical Behavior

You may know people who do one thing one day and do the opposite the next, who change their minds and directions depending on who talked to them last, and who swing back and forth between one ineffective behavior and another. The effect on others around (or under) them is highly disruptive. They do not stimulate high performance in themselves or in anyone else. Similarly, you may know or have worked in organizations whose leaders take them from one direction to another, chasing every fad and seeming "opportunity" coming down the road, tearing these companies apart in the process.

A person can express paradoxical qualities in negative ways. When this happens, the person flip-flops, or in our language, "swings back and forth between" the two sides of the paradox. In chapter 5 we use a pendulum as a diagnostic tool to help people understand when they are acting negatively and what to do to change their behavior. Jerry Fletcher is the developer of this tool, so years ago it was dubbed "Fletcher's Pendulum."

Two Illustrative Examples

To illustrate the process of Paradoxical Thinking, we have chosen two examples from our years of consulting practice. One client, whom we call Renee, was struggling to make a decision between staying in her current job, which seemed to offer a stable income but little chance to advance and grow, or going out on her own to create a very different kind of business. The second, whom we call John, was a manager who was struggling to get good results out of a very talented but difficult employee. Both were frustrated and angry that their problems would not yield to their usual combination of intelligence and effort. They were in negative cycles where everything they did seemed to make the problems worse.

We will use "Renee" and "John" to illustrate the five steps of Paradoxical Thinking. As we discuss their situations, we will provide more detail about their use of the process to demonstrate how to apply the steps yourself. To a high degree the examples used in this book are real. However, we have changed many details and combined examples of more than one person to illustrate some aspects of the process. We have also occasionally modified or simplified the actual example to make the process stand out more sharply.

Meet "Renee"

Renee Stein earned a Stanford MBA and over the past decade had risen to a middle management level in a large bank. As part of a small, highly expert team that traveled a great deal, she participated in investigations of proposed mergers and acquisitions. After its investigation, the team would recommend whether the bank should participate in the funding.

The work was challenging, though she had been part of enough investigations that there was little new to experience. She was one of the higher ranking women in the bank, and the only woman on the mergers and acquisitions team, but her boss and everyone above him were men. Although she had a solid working relationship with her boss, she felt pretty much at a dead end in her career.

For years she had a weekend business of providing flower arrangements for her friends' parties, weddings, funerals, and other occasions. She loved the work and had more business than she could handle. All of her clients recommended her to their friends.

She used her expertise with spreadsheets to develop a sophisticated analytic program so she could bid on jobs and adjust her bids for the different prices of flowers. When she substituted one type flower for another, depending on what looked best at the wholesale market, she could immediately calculate her costs and margins. She felt her financial expertise gave her a competitive advantage in the floral design business.

She had gradually begun to consider quitting her job at the bank and operating her floral design business full time. Since she had prepared pro forma profit and loss statements, she knew how much business she would have to attract to make a living and even had a pretty detailed marketing plan.

The floral design business was attractive to Renee. There would be no travel. She would be doing something she knew she loved. She would be a critical part of important events in people's lives, something she knew would provide more immediate and tangible emotional satisfaction than working on corporate mergers. On the downside, the paycheck would be uncertain, there would be few perks, the work would involve long hours, and somehow it seemed that she wouldn't be doing justice to her Stanford MBA managing a flower business.

So, despite all the preparatory work, she seemed unable to make a decision about whether to stay at the bank or to leave and try the floral design business. One day she would be certain she was leaving; the next she would get some accolades from her boss or teammates and wonder how she could even consider resigning. She felt increasingly frustrated and hopeless about resolving her dilemma. She was afraid that some day, just to end the tension, she would give up on the idea of running her own business and then wonder for years whether she did the right thing. She wanted to make a clean decision, not one driven by frustration.

Meet "John"

Our second example, John, comes from our association with the director of marketing for a major U.S. consumer products firm. He had successfully guided marketing developments in the United States and a dozen other countries for more than a decade. He was an experienced manager who directed a staff of twenty. Trained as an accountant, John had previously served as the finance director for a clothing distribution corporation. He understood the requirements of his company's bureaucracy, as well as his customers' needs, and was respected by his superiors and staff.

For six months before we began to work with him, John had been increasingly irritated and angered by his newest employee, Arthur. Arthur had been recruited after an extensive search. While John regarded himself as a good, experienced manager, he did not seem to be able to "manage" Arthur well. Arthur was young, full of talent, and as explosive as John was steady. When given an assignment and turned loose, Arthur would plunge into it with massive energy, but his judgment was weak. He particularly resisted the methodical attention to detail that a financial job required even though he was a trained accountant.

Just the previous month, John had given Arthur the job of visiting various regional offices and training people in the new time-tracking and accounting system that was being implemented company wide. Despite John's emphasizing to Arthur how important it was for everyone to follow the same procedures for inputting data, Arthur, an admitted computer whiz, had actually modified the program at a number of sites to accommodate differences in what the offices wanted to input. The result was a hodge-podge of data that couldn't be aggregated properly. Furious, John had confronted Arthur, only to end up in a shouting match when Arthur insisted he had improved a lousy system. Later Arthur relented and admitted he shouldn't have made unauthorized changes, but John still had to pay for the additional trips to the sites to do the job properly.

Unfortunately, this wasn't the first of Arthur's efforts that ended up requiring extra work by someone else to clean up his mistakes—only the most damaging. John admired Arthur's energy, his intelligence, and his drive to make things better. He just couldn't find a way to reign him in without causing an explosion. Furthermore, it was taking too much of his time. Either he had to find a way to manage Arthur that took less of his time or he would have to let Arthur go—a decision that he did not desire to make.

Conclusion

The following chapters will explain how you can use Paradoxical Thinking to solve your problems and produce breakthrough results, particularly with respect to issues that currently seem to have no solution. We will use the stories of Renee and John to illustrate how they came to understand their personal paradoxes and use them to produce the results they wanted. The tools described in these case examples will enable you to apply the concepts yourself, using your own paradoxical qualities to achieve goals more effectively.

SUMMARY OF KEY POINTS

✓ This book uses the term "paradox" to mean contradictory or *seemingly* impossible combinations of ideas or actions. The impossibility refers to a person's own limited frame of reference that prevents him or her from producing a creative resolution to a dilemma.

✓ Each person has a particular combination of contradictory and paradoxical qualities that seem to work together to produce that person's best work.

✓ The power of paradox is that each side of the contradiction can be equally dominant and seem to be present simultaneously: the result is not a compromise as the apparent contradiction would seem to require, but rather, both sides are present fully.

✓ Paradoxical Thinking describes the process of bringing together consciously the two paradoxical sides of yourself to achieve outstanding results.

✓ Paradoxical Thinking involves five steps:

1. Finding Your Core Personal Paradox

2. Perception-Shifting

3. Defining Your Problem Situation and Setting Your Goal

4. Rating Yourself on Fletcher's Pendulum

5. Choosing Action Steps to Improve Your Self-Ratings

✓ The route to sustaining high performance is to consciously and actively encourage yourself to be paradoxical.

2

Finding Your Core Personal Paradox

The curious paradox is that when I accept myself just as I am, then I can change.

— CARL ROGERS

The starting point—Step 1 of the five-step Paradoxical Thinking process—is to find your core personal paradox. This step has three parts:

Step 1. Finding Your Core Personal Paradox

    1a. List your personal qualities and characteristics

    1b. Combine these personal qualities and characteristics into paradoxical pairs using oxymorons

    1c. Select one combination that describes a central conflict or tension you struggle with

We will illustrate each part of Step 1 using the Renee and John examples. Then we suggest you apply the process to yourself.

1a. List Your Personal Qualities and Characteristics

The first thing to do is very simple: make a list of your varied qualities and characteristics. Try to think of at least twenty. The list should contain both positive and negative qualities. Here are some suggestions to help generate a list:

» Start with types of actions you like to take and roles you like to play. For example, long-range planner, risktaker, conformist, competitor, rule-maker, or sympathizer.

» Then list words or phrases that would be used to describe you by people who know you: your spouse, best friend, your boss, a customer. For example, friendly, truthful, reliable, source of new ideas, synthesizer, devil's advocate, optimist.

» Finally, list words or phrases that would be used to describe you by someone who knows you well and who doesn't like you particularly: a former spouse, a neighbor with whom you didn't get along, an investor in a company you ran that did poorly, the plaintiff in a lawsuit against you. For example, self-doubter, procrastinator, self-serving, nasty, deceptive, airhead, or unscrupulous.

» If you have an important characteristic in mind but no one or two word phrase can capture it, use several words. For example, "hard to pin down," "challenger of the status quo," or "smoother of ruffled feathers" might capture an aspect of you more precisely.

It is important that you not reject descriptive words or phrases that you dislike. If a word could be used by you or someone else, even in a small way, to describe you, jot it down at this point. Finding something positive about personal qualities you may have spent a lifetime disliking or even repressing is actually the key to increased personal productivity and satisfaction. As the process continues, you will have ample opportunity to delete, edit, and combine descriptive words in a variety of ways.

When you finish your list, mark with a star "✳" the words or phrases on the list that describe qualities you like about yourself, and mark with an X the qualities that you dislike.

Let us illustrate with Renee and John.

Renee's List of Characteristics

Renee made a list of as many of her own qualities as she could, both positive and negative. She described herself as others might describe her, such as her best friend, her boss, her parents, or her worst enemies.

A long list of traits emerged. Nearly every description was accompanied by a brief story describing how the trait was expressed in her life or why someone she knew would say that of her. We told Renee not to delete the qualities that were uncomfortable for her to acknowledge. We reassured her that we would help her find the positive expressions of any qualities she disliked.

She then marked her list according to which characteristics she liked and which she disliked. This was Renee's marked list:

Careful	*	Self-Doubting	X
Take-Charge	*	Risktaker	*
Insecure	X	Creative	*
Overachiever	*	Distinct	*
Talented	*	Follower	X
Cautious	X	Meticulous	*
Vague	X	Hands-On	*
Goal-Directed	*	Analytical	*
Tolerant	*	Indecisive	X
Bravado	*	Service-Oriented	*
Pensive	*	Dependable	*
Fun	*	Restrained	X

Note that she included on the list the words "insecure," "self-doubting," "cautious," "vague," "restrained," and "indecisive." She didn't like these, but they were true of her—at least at times and in the eyes of some people who knew her—so she put them down.

John's List of Characteristics

John was confused initially that the route to dealing with Arthur better was to look at himself. He assumed the process would be focused on getting Arthur to change. However, when a relationship is in trouble and you want someone else to change, there is usually something wrong with how you are approaching the problem. In some way, John was not engaging both sides of his paradoxical nature. If he were, the relationship would be working better. He needed to look first at his own behavior.

Following the same steps we outlined for Renee, John listed a wide variety of personal characteristics he felt described him and that he imagined others would say in describing him. Here is John's marked list:

Boring	X	Dull	X
Straight-Laced	X	Rule-Follower	*
Clumsy	X	Disciplined	*
Methodical	*	Colorless	X
Steady	*	Honest	*
Trustworthy	*	Good Follower	*
Caring	*	Friendly	*
Extroverted	*	Detailed	*
Do It Right	*	Approachable	*
Pushover	X	Concerned	*

Notice that John included words like "boring," "dull," "colorless," and "clumsy," even though he disliked them. They were true about him, at least in the eyes of some people who knew him, and he knew that at times they were accurate.

It's Your Turn

Now you try it. Make a list of as many varied positive and negative characteristics as you can. When you have listed at least twenty characteristics, mark with a star "*" the ones you particularly like about yourself. Don't delete the ones you dislike, just mark them with an X. When you have finished your list, go on to the next section.

1b. Combine These Personal Qualities and Characteristics into Paradoxical Pairs Using Oxymorons

Once you have identified your many characteristics—some of which you may view positively and others you may view negatively—some paradoxical combination of them holds the key to your own high performance. To determine which one, make as many paradoxical combinations as you can using the items on your list of characteristics. Typically, most of the pairs include one "positive" and one "negative" characteristic. In creating the pairs, keep in mind the quality that the word is trying to capture. Make sure the underlying personal qualities are opposites. Don't just mechanically combine words.

Oxymorons: A Short Diversion

We have found over the years that using *oxymorons* is a good way to help our clients understand the phenomenon of paradox. Thus we are going to take a short diversion here to explain the concept of oxymorons.

An oxymoron is defined as:

> A combination of apparently contradictory words or phrases which describe a "paradoxical truth."

Oxymorons are quite prevalent in our society. "Plastic glasses," "jumbo shrimp," and "original replacement parts" are just a few examples. Adults who have become familiar with oxymorons often humorously consider the seeming impossibility of "military intelligence," "bureaucratic efficiency," and a "liberal republican."

The advertising industry uses the oxymoron to capture human attention. They know that when the brain is ambling along reading something and it hits an oxymoron, it comes to a screeching halt: Something is not right here! In the seconds it takes your brain to readjust to the paradoxical image an oxymoron presents, your attention has been captured. For example, when a form of packaging was invented to prevent dehydration and decomposition of foods stored in electric freezers, advertisers came up with the oxymoron "freezer burn" to describe the problem the packaging would solve.

Using an oxymoron to label your own paradoxical qualities can be very helpful in that it "personifies" the inherent conflict or tension between the two sides of your core personal paradox. For example, a successful entrepreneur described herself as a "hesitant risktaker." As an entrepreneur she took risks all the time in her business yet each one was taken carefully; she did not engage in risks capriciously. She evaluated her possible actions and the risks very carefully before she committed herself.

Her understanding of the fact that she was *both* a risktaker and hesitant (or careful) in the way she took risks helped her understand the contradictory qualities that together made her a successful entrepreneur.

After our work with her, she understood that rather than try to choose between her two contradictory natures, she could best sustain her success as an entrepreneur by utilizing both—being willing to take risks as an essential part of maintaining a successful business and being as careful as she could be before committing to do so.

In another example, a staff manager in a large government operation realized a perfect way to describe himself when he was at his best was as a "silken sergeant." When he managed his people best, he was tough like a drill sergeant, but he did it in a gentle, smiling, inoffensively "silken" way, which worked well. He was highly respected by his employees who understood and liked both his toughness and his gentle expression of it.

It is helpful to think of an oxymoron as a combination of an adjective and a noun that describes a type of person. Take for example, "silken sergeant," "spontaneous planner," "hesitant risktaker," or "gentle warrior." The nouns—"sergeant," "planner," "risktaker," and "warrior"—are words that name a type of person. An adjective answers the question What kind of person is it?—a *silken* sergeant, a *spontaneous* planner, a *hesitant* risktaker, a *gentle* warrior.

Here are some oxymorons that participants developed for themselves in our workshops. Visualize both sides of the paradox described by the oxymoron and try to imagine what sort of person it might describe. Can you think of people you know who could be described by using any of these oxymorons?

Attack Sheep	Well-Organized Slob
Lazy Do-It-All	Velvet Jackhammer
Competent Self-Doubter	Insecure Tower-of-Strength
Spontaneous Planner	Happy-Go-Lucky Jackal
Ruthless Helper	I'll-Do-It-My-Way Conformist
Self-Assured Bowl-of-Jelly	Cutthroat Pussycat
Passionate Robot	Ambitious Slowpoke
Hard-Working Dreamer	Gentle Warrior
Creative Imitator	Assertive Doormat
Determined Wanderer	Iron-Willed Pussycat
Hesitant Risktaker	Vacationing Workaholic
Toothless Shark	Iron Butterfly

Using the two examples of Renee and John, we will illustrate the process of part 1b.

Renee Creates Her List of Personal Oxymorons

We asked Renee to combine the descriptive words on her list into pairs that seemed to be contradictory, or oxymoronic. When she did this, she dropped many of the words, as they either didn't make contradictory combinations, or they didn't seem to capture a core paradox with which she struggled.

She also changed the words slightly into a combination of an adjective describing a noun. Here are the pairs she chose:

Careful Risktaker

Self-Doubting Overachiever

Vague Analyst

Meticulous Tolerator

Take-Charge Namby-Pamby

John Creates His List of Personal Oxymorons

John identified the qualities on his list that appeared to be contradictory or paradoxical. Changing the format into a combination of an adjective describing a noun, here are the pairs he chose:

Rigid Nice Guy

Conventional Extrovert

Approachable Do-It-Righter

Dominating Good-Follower

Open-Minded Rule-Follower

It's Your Turn

Create as many personal oxymorons from your list of qualities and characteristics as you can. Make sure that each one captures truthfully two opposite qualities you have that are often in conflict and tension. A long list is helpful, though most people can create only four or five pairs.

1c. Select One Combination That Describes a Central Conflict or Tension You Struggle With

The final part of Step 1 is to pick a particular oxymoron that resonates with you, that seems to describe a core personal conflict with which you struggle. It should be one that makes you a little uncomfortable to acknowledge because in your heart of hearts you know that it's true. You should be able to tell a story or give an example of how it shows up in your life.

Renee Selects Her Core Personal Paradox

We asked Renee to pick one oxymoron from her list as her core personal paradox—the one that had the deepest meaning for her. We told her to consider the following questions: Which pair seemed most familiar, yet insightful? Which combination of words was emotionally charged for her? What words reflected the core conflict or tension she kept trying to manage in her life?

Renee selected "self-doubting overachiever" as her core personal paradox. Renee felt it identified the contradictory qualities with which she had often struggled in the past, particularly when she tried to overcome or eliminate her self-doubting nature. She told several stories of times she had taken on a difficult assignment, experienced tremendous self-doubt, drove herself unmercifully, and ended up with a result that was way beyond what she ever imagined she could achieve—yet she still doubted herself. It seemed like no achievement ever extinguished her self-doubt.

She was somewhat relieved to learn that she might not have to continue the struggle between self-doubt and over achievement, but she was also somewhat skeptical. Ultimately, using Paradoxical Thinking, she learned to take advantage of her tendency toward overachieving and to see the virtue in her intense self-doubting.

In the following chapters, we will show how Renee came to understand the "self-doubting overachiever" part of herself and how this understanding helped her to resolve her dilemma about staying with the bank or going out on her own and starting a floral design business.

John Selects His Core Personal Paradox

John picked the oxymoron "conventional extrovert" as his core personal paradox. It reflected the principal contradiction of his life: his drive to be "out there" (extroverted) and his tendency to "blend into the woodwork" (conventional).

Ultimately, as the following chapters will show, he learned to take advantage of his extroverted qualities and to see the virtue in his tendency toward being dull and conventional. He was also able to connect this core personal paradox to resolving his problem with Arthur.

While we asked Renee and John to pick only one oxymoron as their core personal paradox, it is a good idea to retain the other oxymoron combinations that seem true and insightful. You can refer back to them later. Often it turns out that the other oxymoron combinations on your list are "variations on the same theme" as your selected core personal paradox. Many times at the end of the Paradoxical Thinking process, or after using the process a number of times, people are able to create a new oxymoron that captures the core personal paradox even better. The other examples on your list can help in this.

Other Examples

Here are a few oxymorons that other people we have worked with have chosen as their core personal paradoxes:

» A company's ombudsperson is attracted by conflict and also pursues harmony and "quiet time" at work and at home. She marches into conflicts, excited by the prospect of "refereeing a good fight," but she seeks a long-lasting resolution. She described herself as a "harmony-loving conflict-seeker."

» A manager is capable of stepping into the middle of a hostile situation and convincing people to do what he wants them to do, yet he can be unwilling to return something he bought at a store and doesn't like because he just doesn't want the hassle. He described himself as a "timid turnaround-specialist."

» A successful product designer does what it takes to succeed, paying careful attention to detail, yet she can be blithely unconcerned about others' reactions to what she does and immune to pressure. She described herself as a "compulsive free spirit."

» A very busy corporate executive does every job virtually by himself, yet he considers himself lazy. When he is lazy, it gives him time to think, weigh competing projects, and take time to be with his family. He described himself as a "lazy do-it-all."

It's Your Turn

Picking an Oxymoron as Your Core Personal Paradox Some of the oxymorons you have developed may sound interesting, even funny, but may not really be true of you. Discard those that don't capture some truth about yourself. Pick the one combination in which both words or phrases are true and capture a core personal conflict or tension with which you seem to be constantly struggling. Rework it if you need to so that you have an adjective-noun pair.

Describing How It Shows Up All of the people who named their inherent contradictions with one of the oxymorons above were able to describe in some short story how each side showed up in their lives. The sense of humor reflected in many of them shows the refreshing spirit human beings can bring to facing difficult aspects of themselves. Giving a humorous name to aspects of ourselves that we find unpleasant or embarrassing lowers the barriers to learning to use them positively.

Suggestions and Caveats

Selecting a Core Personal Paradox and Creating an Oxymoron

Here are a few suggestions to help you create a personal oxymoron that captures vividly, and often with humor, the core personal paradox you feel you have:

» Invent Words or Phrases. It is often helpful to "invent" words and phrases. For example, if you identify that you often smooth the ruffled feathers of other people, you might write "feather-smoother."

» Use Names of Animals. It's often helpful and fun when describing yourself to use an animal name. For example, if you are powerful and fearless, you might say you are "lion-hearted." If you are shy or timid, you might call yourself a "mouse."

» Look for Combinations of Words on Your List That Are Already Opposites. One or more of these might resonate as capturing a core personal conflict or tension you struggle with.

» Elaborate on the Words or Phrases on Your List. For example, you might have "original thinker" one place on the list and "rigid" in another place. As you consider these words and phrases, the "rigid" characteristic might really be a belief that everything has to be done exactly right. If so, you might write "original-thinking stickler-for-details" as a possible oxymoron for yourself.

» Think Metaphorically. It is helpful to think metaphorically. For example, if two of your words are "meek" and "powerful," you might come up with "wallflower lioness" as an oxymoron.

» Use Historical, Fictional and Famous People. It is fine to use a fictional, historical, or famous character as an opposite. For example, if you wrote "laid-back" and "tough" on your list, you might use "laid-back Attila the Hun" or "laid-back Godzilla" as your oxymoron. Or if you put "emotional" and "focused" in the column, you might write "emotional Mr. Spock" (from *Star Trek*) as your oxymoron.

» Use Humor. We encourage you to use humor. As a matter of fact, humor works very well in this process. For example, if you had among the words you wrote on your list "serious" and "slapstick," you might put "slapstick mortician" as your oxymoron.

» Beware of Overly "Nice" Lists. Write down things your enemies, your ex-spouses, or your competitors might use to describe you, just to get possibilities on the list that you might not normally write. This is vitally important. If your initial list is too simplistic or politically correct, the resulting paradoxes will lack the gutsy reality that leads to unique, personal insights. To describe yourself as a "table-banging wall flower," if it's true, is a lot better than something watered down like "assertive gentle person." You can use either one, but the more raw and gutsy, the better.

» Eschew Logical Opposites. Beware of creating paradoxes just by putting down the logical opposite of some of the descriptive words. Our experience suggests that logical opposites rarely describe the uniqueness of a person. They are too easy to choose without having to think about it carefully. "Warm-hearted" might be a good descriptor of you. Its opposite, "cold-hearted," probably isn't. The personal paradox that fits you might be something more like "warm-hearted battering ram" or "warm-hearted judge."

» Pick Opposites That Are "Uncomfortably" True. The important thing is to pick a pair of opposites that are both true of you. Let's say you are, for example, a "cold-blooded humorist." You can identify with the cold-blooded side and feel that part of yourself. You know how that side expresses itself. You also know and feel the humorist side of yourself.

» Accept Characteristics You Initially Resist. Many times people "know" that one characteristic is true of them, but they are afraid it might shatter their self-image if they admit it. We remember distinctly one woman who described herself as a "supportive bitch." She said bluntly that she had spent a lot of her life creating an image that she was supportive, motherly, and caring, but she also had her bitchy side. She could be incredibly judgmental and demanding about the way things "should" be. When she finally admitted this to herself, she was able to gain some particularly powerful insights about how to use her "bitchy" side in constructive and useful ways. She also found ways to be supportive that didn't involve being a doormat. It was a tremendous relief to break the stereotyped image she felt she had to maintain.

» Let Multiple Oxymorons Settle. Many times people find several oxymorons that seem to apply to them. Our record is thirty-four; five or six initial ones is common. If a number seem equally true and you find it difficult to choose just one, keep the whole list in front of you for a day or so. Usually, a number of the oxymorons are variations on a theme, and after letting them all settle, you will be able to select one or create a new one that is the essence of the large list.

Discomfort with One Side

If you are like most people, you will be uncomfortable with some of the characteristics you have listed about yourself. Once you choose an oxymoron, you may be less comfortable with one side of it than the other. If you were to describe yourself as the "silken sergeant," you might not like your tough, get-things-done qualities. You might prefer getting things done in a more gentle, "silken" way. If you accurately described yourself as a "compulsive free spirit," perhaps you don't like your "compulsive" tendencies.

If one side of your core personal paradox seems like a limitation, you probably have felt for much of your life that you "shouldn't" act that way, or you would be "better off" if you were different. It is likely that you have tried to suppress or eliminate that quality of your personality. Yet this is not the direction to go.

Rather, when people are at their best, they embrace the contradictions inherent in their core personal paradox. They

» embody both sides of the contradictory tendencies in their paradox

» express those qualities in a mature, positive, and healthy form

Just as for Renee and John, *the issue for you is to find the mature, healthy, and positive expression of your contradictory qualities and learn how to keep both of them present simultaneously.*

SUMMARY OF KEY POINTS

✓ People perform their best work when they learn to embrace and express simultaneously their paradoxical qualities.

✓ An oxymoron is defined as a combination of apparently contradictory words or phrases that describes a "paradoxical truth."

✓ Using an oxymoron to describe your own paradoxical qualities is very helpful because it names in a truthful and easy-to-relate-to manner the tensions you are trying to deal with in your own life.

✓ The three-part process for determining your core personal paradox is as follows:

1a. List your personal qualities and characteristics

1b. Combine these personal qualities and characteristics into paradoxical pairs using oxymorons

1c. Select one combination that describes a central conflict or tension you struggle with

✓ If one side of your core personal paradox seems like a limitation, it is likely that you have tried to suppress or eliminate that quality of your personality. The key is to find the mature, healthy and positive expression of your contradictory qualities.

✓ Avoid overly "nice" lists and logical opposites when determining your personal oxymoron.

3

Perception-Shifting

*Once upon a time a man whose ax was missing suspected
his neighbor's son. The boy walked like a thief, looked like
a thief, and spoke like a thief. But the man found his ax
while digging in the valley, and the next time he saw his
neighbor's son, the boy walked, looked, and spoke like any
other child.*

— LAO-TZU

The next step—Step 2 of the five-step Paradoxical Thinking
process—is to expand your understanding of your core personal paradox. In this step you will work directly with the oxymoron you selected.
You will be asked to expand your perceptions and judgments about the
positive or negative value of your paradoxical qualities. This step—
which we call Perception-Shifting—has six parts:

Step 2. Perception-Shifting

2a. List positives of preferred side

35

2b. List negatives of preferred side

2c. List negatives of disliked side

2d. List positives of disliked side

2e. Choose a High Performance Oxymoron

2f. Choose a Nightmare Oxymoron

Perception-Shifting: An Introduction

Many of you will have an initial tendency to like one side of your core personal paradox much better than the other, or even to dislike both sides. So long as you do, you won't want to utilize both sides simultaneously. At least one of the sides will be judged as negative and either suppressed or expressed in a negative and sometimes destructive form. Until you are able to see the value of both sides and know how to express those qualities to achieve that value, you will not understand how to use your paradoxical qualities to help reach your goals.

Characteristics that everyone agrees are negative are the extreme form of qualities that can be positive and constructive if utilized correctly. You need to be cautious about trying to suppress or eliminate qualities in yourself that you believe are negative or about trying to change yourself entirely. A better and faster path is to learn to control them and use these qualities in some positive way.

Regardless of your characteristics, regardless of the hand you have been dealt by the accidents of birth, genetics, and opportunity, your personal qualities can be seen in a positive light and used in a mature and effective way to achieve results. The objective of this chapter is to amplify your understanding of what combinations of traits and their manner of expression lead to your greatest effectiveness.

Labels and Self-Judgment

When you become aware of and dislike a personal quality, you will label it with a word that carries loaded, negative connotations. That label then reinforces your negative judgment, making it difficult to see the positive possibilities.

For example, if you are admittedly disheveled and scattered, you might label yourself a "slob." If you do, the label's connotations will limit your ability to see any positive personal strengths that might result from your "slob-like" tendencies. You could not imagine calling on your "slob-like" qualities to achieve something positive, and therefore the likelihood that anyone else would call upon these qualities to help them seems equally remote.

Now assume you don't try to "do" anything about this quality of yourself. Just change the word you use to label this aspect from "slob" to "disorganized." This reduces the negative connotations and might enable you to judge yourself less harshly, seeing yourself as having more capabilities than you thought. However, it's still difficult to see how "disorganized" can be a virtue.

Now, again, assume you don't change at all. This time change the label for this "slob-like" aspect of yourself from "disorganized" to "relatively impervious to societal and organizational pressure to organize my life and work space a certain way." Now you might see some of the positives of your "slob-like" qualities. The very lack of concern for social convention that allows you to live and act as a slob if you choose to can be understood as an ability to withstand social pressure to conform. In certain situations this is invaluable, especially when the success of some activity depends on resisting pressure to achieve a quick payoff and instead building for a longer-term, more valuable result.

Different labels for the same quality can be arranged on a simple scale from the most negative and unflattering (and therefore least likely to be used effectively) to the most positive and eye-opening. We find it convenient to use a 200-point scale, from minus 100 (−100) through zero (0) to plus 100 (+100), so we can easily talk about how far up or down the scale a particular label is:

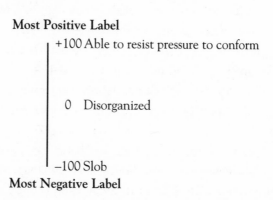

Most Positive Label

+100 Able to resist pressure to conform

0 Disorganized

−100 Slob

Most Negative Label

If you have already judged yourself to be a "slob," you will enter into a variety of situations already locked into a particularly limited mind-set—sloppy, undisciplined, unkempt, uncaring, low self-esteem. You will be less prepared to act effectively. However, if you have recognized that you have "an ability to resist pressure to conform," your capacity to act effectively can be much greater.

Just as qualities you judge as negative have positive forms of expression, ones you judge as positive can have quite negative expressions. A positive label can blind you to its downside. Understanding the negative, immature expressions of the side of your core personal paradox that you like is as important as seeing the positives of something about yourself that you dislike.

Let's say you have a strong tendency to set goals and drive yourself and others to achieve them. It might be quite reasonable to label that characteristic "leadership." However, the same qualities that bring about effective leadership can get out of control and drift over the line into being autocratic and dictatorial. Labeling yourself as a "leader" may blind you to feedback that people are resisting, or going along sullenly with your directions, and you are no longer really an effective leader.

You need to recognize that leadership qualities can be expressed in a negative way, and you should be alert to the signals that you are no longer using this strength positively. This awareness can correct potential negative consequences long before there is an explosion of resistance.

We See What We Believe

The human predilection toward locking into a particular viewpoint and then seeing the entire world that way is not new. Many studies on how human belief systems operate have shattered the notion that we believe what we see. For the most part, we see what we believe, and it is hard for any perception to change the belief. It's much easier to deny information that doesn't fit our beliefs. For example, if you believe a certain group of people is good, you will see goodness in those people. If you believe a human quality or behavior is good, you will have the tendency to see only goodness when that behavior is encountered. Similarly, if you believe something about you is bad, you will be hard pressed to find anything positive about it. Even when you use the quality in a positive way, there will be the tendency to deny its value.

If you become locked into a viewpoint and make assumptions about "how things are" in the landscape of your life, your individual experiences will start to have less and less impact. Almost regardless of what happens, you will keep your previously established beliefs. Your beliefs and ways of thinking and acting become habitual, rote, and mechanical. You are then blinded to the variations and possibilities that exist within a situation, leading to serious overreaction and missed opportunities. Conversely, other people can lock into a particularly limited view of *your* capabilities, or expect you to behave in only stereotyped ways, and it can be terribly difficult to break out of the mental box they have placed you in.

Breaking Out of Narrow, Preconceived Judgments

What is really true about people is that every characteristic embodies potentially good and bad, positive and negative, mature and immature aspects. The challenge is understanding and using your capabilities in positive, mature, and constructive ways rather than suppressing the qualities you don't like or expressing them in negative ways. Unless you are able to break your preconceived notions—change your self-labels— you will never fully appreciate your capabilities and be willing to work toward using them positively.

The story that heads this chapter of the man who lost his ax reflects the danger of maintaining belief systems without question: they keep us from creatively resolving a problem or a difficult situation. It also takes a great deal of energy to maintain a view of a situation that is basically inaccurate—energy that could be better used to resolve the predicament. How many times have you misspent energy because you insisted on holding onto a belief that did not, in the long run, serve you or make the situation better?

Perception-Shifting: An Exercise

To help you recognize that very few things are inherently good or bad (despite people's penchant for assigning "right/wrong" values to them), consider the following exercise that we did with various groups of people over a period of a year. Individuals in the groups were asked to free-associate the meaning of "energetic," "honest," and "leader." Below is a composite set of their associations, all of them positive:

Initial Positive Associations

↑ fun	↑ credible	↑ guide
doer	genuine	pilot
lively	upright	initiative
intense	righteous	instigator
passionate	respectable	influencer
enthusiastic	trustworthy	command
enterprising	honorable	committed
		exemplary
+	+	+
(positives)	(positives)	(positives)
Energetic	**Honest**	**Leader**

We found that the groups had fun finding these associations, and they did it quickly.

Coming up with the negative, or immature aspects of these same qualities, however, was typically much more difficult. If you have the predisposition toward thinking these words are "good," how can things get "off track" with these qualities? What happens when these qualities begin to "go wrong"? The key to understanding how "good" qualities go bad is to focus on how they are expressed in the *extreme*.

When we asked people in the groups to describe the extreme form of these positive qualities, they discovered that there is a larger picture than just the positive associations they had seen.

Newly Perceived Negative Associations

Energetic	**Honest**	**Leader**
(negatives)	(negatives)	(negatives)
-	-	-
overwhelming	overly disclosing	overshadowing
energy drain	self-righteous	self-important
to deal with	"better than"	superiority
insensitive	inflexible	dominating
steamroller	obsessive	frightening
frenetic ↓	↓	↓

Almost everyone had had the experience of knowing someone who could accurately be described by the negative or immature version of these three characteristics.

A similar phenomenon occurs when people have negative associations with particular words or ideas and fail to see the positive aspects. We asked the same groups to free-associate the meaning of "steamroller," "crude," and "wimp," and in this case all of their words were negative:

Initial Negative Associations

Steamroller	Crude	Wimp
(negatives)	(negatives)	(negatives)
-	-	-
self-absorbed	thoughtless	ineffectual
domineering	insensitive	doormat
blind and deaf	unrefined	fearful
overbearing	uncaring	passive
threatening	abrasive	coward
removed	coarse	worrier
brutish	rough	weak
	gross	
	raw	

Through social and family conditioning, people come to believe that anyone who could be described using one of these three words is undesirable. Almost everyone can recall an experience of either dealing with someone like this or acting like this themselves, and feeling angry if they were the recipient of the label.

In our view, however, when people are acting in the way described by the words listed under "steamroller," for example, they are expressing *the negative extremes* of "steamroller." Experiencing someone acting like a steamroller toward you brings up your defenses. If people have a tendency to steamroll others and want to become more effective, they often try to tone down that part of themselves or eliminate it. However, eliminating an inherent aspect of one's nature is extremely difficult. A more efficient and effective process is to learn how that same characteristic might be expressed positively.

We then asked the groups to come up with positive associations to the same words. Most people found it enlightening to discover that there is a broader, more positive picture to their own, initially biased associations. Here's a composite picture from a number of the different groups:

Newly Perceived Positive Associations

↑	↑	↑
driver	real	soft
strong	natural	gentle
charger	pristine	careful
efficient	untouched	moderate
fearless	pragmatic	noncombative
powerful	unconcerned	unthreatening
take charge	tell-it-like-it-is	wants to be sure
action-oriented	straightforward	doesn't take sides
gets things done		
+	+	+
(positives)	(positives)	(positives)
Steamroller	**Crude**	**Wimp**

Once you realize that positive expressions exist for each of the behaviors identified by these words, you can then alter your way of viewing real people whom you had previously placed into these negative categories. You can develop more effective relationships by focusing your attention on these positive possibilities.

As you can see, the whole picture is not inherently positive or negative but embodies both possibilities. The question is whether the person who has the characteristic has control of it and has learned to use it in a positive way.

Full Perception-Shifted Perspective on Three "Positive" Words

	upright	
fun	credible	guide
doer	genuine	pilot
lively	honorable	initiative
"live wire"	principled	instigator
intense	righteous	influencer
passionate	respectable	command
enthusiastic	trustworthy	committed
enterprising	honorable	exemplary
+	+	+
	(Positive, Mature Expressions)	
Energetic	**Honest**	**Leader**
	(Negative, Extreme Expressions)	
-	-	-
overwhelming	overly disclosing	self-important
energy-sucker	self-righteous	overshadowing
insensitive	"better than"	superiority
forceful	inflexible	dominating
frenetic	obsessive	frightening

Full Perception-Shifted Perspective on Three "Negative" Words

driver		
strong	real	soft
charger	natural	gentle
efficient	pristine	careful
fearless	untouched	moderate
powerful	pragmatic	unthreatening
take charge	unconcerned	noncombative
action-oriented	tell-it-like-it-is	wants to be sure
gets things done	straightforward	doesn't take sides
+	+	+
	(Positive, Mature Expressions)	
Steamroller	**Crude**	**Wimp**
	(Negative, Extreme Expressions)	
-	-	-
self-absorbed	thoughtless	ineffectual
domineering	insensitive	doormat
blind and deaf	unrefined	fearful
overbearing	uncaring	passive
threatening	abrasive	coward
removed	coarse	worrier
brutish	rough	weak
	gross	
	raw	

Perception-Shifting Renee's Core Personal Paradox

Renee selected "self-doubting overachiever" as an oxymoron that described her core personal paradox. How can Renee begin to alter her perceptions and judgments about herself so that she doesn't limit her thinking and can take the greatest advantage of her unique qualities?

Positives of Renee's Preferred Side

Renee began Perception-Shifting her oxymoron starting with the characteristic of the oxymoron that she liked best—"overachiever." It was easy for Renee to describe positive ways this quality might be expressed. She asked herself, what is a person like who uses her overachiever tendency in a mature, constructive way? What contribution is that person making? What's "good" about being an overachiever? Renee came up with this list:

Positive Expressions of an Overachiever Tendency

leader
quick acting
a "doer"
self-directing
fearless
effective
productive
focused
exceeds expectations
accomplished
disciplined
does her share (and more)
+
(Positive, Mature Expressions)
Overachiever

Negatives of Renee's Preferred Side

Renee then identified the negative ways in which a person can be an overachiever. The descriptors are listed below. Note that they are not opposites of the overachiever characteristic, but rather extreme forms of it:

Negative Expressions of an Overachiever Tendency

Overachiever
(Negative, Extreme Expressions)
-
compulsive
obsessed
dictatorial
overly demanding
intolerant of others
workaholic
overbearing
prevents others from taking leadership
authoritarian
wheelspinner
misses the subtleties
controlling
does everything herself—never good enough
"win at all costs" attitude

Renee acknowledged that her overachiever tendencies could produce such negative results. She recalled a number of times when she behaved in the negative ways she'd listed. In particular, when things weren't going well, she would tend to become overbearing and authoritarian.

She also recognized that she sometimes did take charge of situations in such a way that other participants never got to practice the skills they needed to be able to take charge themselves. When this happened, the people around Renee would start assuming that she would "handle it." This left a burden on her to follow through and check everyone else's work on top of what was her routinely heavy workload. It was a helpful insight for Renee to see how she both created and perpetuated this problem.

Being an overachiever is not inherently good or bad. It could produce positive or negative results, depending on how well Renee controlled and focused this quality to use it in a positive, mature way. With discipline and focus, the overachiever trait produced great results for Renee. When it was out of control, it produced negative consequences. When Renee saw the expanded view of "overachiever," she was able to foresee where she could inadvertently get "off track" and make preparations to prevent herself from doing so.

Negatives of Renee's Disliked Side

We then turned to the side of Renee that she disliked, which she had labeled "self-doubter" in her oxymoron. Since it was negative already in her perception, we started with the negative.

What was bad about being a self-doubter? In short order she came up with the following list:

Negative Expressions of Self-Doubting

Self-Doubting
(Negative, Extreme Expressions)

-

indecisive
hesitant
loser
excuse-maker
afraid
worried
undecided
confused
unstable
lack of confidence
insecure
always in an uncertain state
hopeless
wimpy
vacillating

It was no wonder Renee hated to think about her self-doubting quality, given these negative associations. However, it is only when self-
doubt is carried to an extreme that it has such negative expressions and
consequences. It isn't inherently bad.

Positives of Renee's Disliked Side

What is the positive value in being a self-doubter? We asked Renee to
say to herself, "I have this characteristic. What would it look like if I
were to begin to express it in its positive form?" She needed to find the
positive expression of "self-doubt" before she could give it a place of
honor in her life and use it in conjunction with her overachiever side.

Renee thought about times when she'd had a self-doubter on her
team who had made an enormously valuable contribution. What could
her self-doubter aspect look like if it was expressed in a mature, healthy,
and constructive way? Renee decided that a positive, mature expression
of "self-doubt" would be:

Positive Expressions of a Self-Doubting Tendency

careful contingency planner
investigates every flaw
accurate in locating pitfalls
detail conscious
prepared
precise
thorough
safety-aware
cautious
protective
look-before-leap
+
(Positive, Mature Expressions)
Self-Doubting

With this expanded viewpoint, Renee was able to see that "self-doubting" was not inherently good or bad. In fact, a self-doubting tendency could be used in quite positive and constructive ways. The good/bad consequence came from judging the way in which she chose to express it. Her self-doubting side encompassed not only the "bad" things she associated with it, but *just as importantly* the "good" qualities that helped her plan for contingencies carefully, that protected her by making sure she "looked before she leapt" when taking risks, and which helped her to maintain her thoroughness and safety-awareness.

She now saw that her self-doubting side served her rather well: it protected her from making decisions before she had enough information. It was her "gate-keeper," the part of herself that ensured she was safe and well prepared. Her task became allowing herself to better and more often express the insecure and self-doubting part of herself in its positive, mature form, rather than in its negative, immature form.

Renee's Choice of a High Performance Oxymoron

Renee then returned to the original idea about paradoxical qualities: that people are most effective when they utilize both sides of their contradictory nature simultaneously. Renee looked over the list of positives for each side and selected the one that best described how she would be expressing that quality when she was most effective:

» At her best as a self-doubter, Renee decided she is "thoroughly prepared."

» At her best as an overachiever, she is an "expectation-exceeder."

Combining these two, Renee at her best is a "thoroughly prepared expectation-exceeder."

This is her High Performance Oxymoron. It is the way in which her contradictory and paradoxical characteristics are expressed when she is most effective.

Renee's Choice of a Nightmare Oxymoron

Renee also identified the worst possible expression of each of the characteristics (her Nightmare Oxymoron), so she could be most attuned to how her core paradoxical qualities might go wrong:

» At her worst as a self-doubter, she feels hopeless.

» At her worst as an overachiever, she is a wheelspinner, redoing work endlessly.

Combining these two, Renee at her worst is a "hopeless wheel-spinner." This is her Nightmare Oxymoron. It is the way in which her contradictory and paradoxical characteristics are expressed when she is most ineffective.

Renee's Perception-Shifting Diagram

Renee's High Performance Oxymoron reminds her of the positive, mature expression of her core personal paradox. If she expresses both sides of her High Performance Oxymoron when taking important actions about people and projects in her life, she will be most effective.

At the same time, her Nightmare Oxymoron reminds her most dramatically of the negative expression of her core personal paradox. When Renee is going to extremes and expressing her Nightmare Oxymoron, she will be more likely to recognize the associated characteristics, and take actions to correct her behavior.

This is Renee's full Perception-Shifting diagram:

Renee's Perception-Shifting Diagram

Thoroughly Prepared Expectation-Exceeder
High Performance Oxymoron

a careful contingency planner	directive
investigating every flaw	quick acting
accurate in locating pitfalls	a "doer"
detail conscious	productive
prepared	self-directed
precise	fearless
thorough	effective
safety aware	leader
cautious	productive
protective	focused
look-before-leap	*exceeds expectations*
	accomplished
	disciplined
	does her share (and more)

+

Self-Doubting   Original Oxymoron   **Overachiever**

+

–   **–**

indecisive	compulsive
hesitant	obsessed
loser	dictatorial
excuse-maker	overly demanding
afraid	intolerant of others
worrier	workaholic
undecided	*wheelspinner*
confused	overbearing
unstable	prevents others from
lack of confidence	leadership skills
insecure	authoritarian
always in an uncertain state	misses the subtleties
hopeless	controlling
wimpy	
vacillating	

Hopeless Wheelspinner
Nightmare Oxymoron

By the time Renee had used Perception-Shifting on her oxymoron, she recognized how limited her thinking had been. She had allowed the characteristics she'd previously deemed negative to work against her, rather than learning to use them creatively and positively to serve her. She also recognized that the characteristics she had always deemed positive could be taken to extremes and then would not work positively for her.

Perception-Shifting John's Core Personal Paradox

John believed both his conventional and his extrovert sides were true. He admitted to a preference toward the extrovert side.

To clarify the positive and negative uses of John's core personal paradox, he used Perception-Shifting to convert "conventional extrovert" into a longer list of positive and negative expressions.

Positives of John's Preferred Side

John found it easy to list the benefits of his extrovert side. Such an individual has these qualities:

Positive Expressions of an Extrovert Tendency

enthused about outside world
friendly
open
good communicator
energetic
fun
good humored
good listener
+
(Positive, Mature Expressions)
Extrovert

Negatives of John's Preferred Side

If John became so extroverted that he was ineffective, he recognized that his behavior could be described as:

Negative Associations of an Extrovert Tendency

Extrovert
(Negative, Extreme Expressions)
-

always talking
always center stage
dominating others
preaching
unconcerned with others' feelings
easily interrupted from work

He could identify times when he had become preachy and dominating. From these associations John saw that being an extrovert wasn't inherently good or bad. It depended on how positively and responsibly he used this personal quality.

Negatives of John's Disliked Side

John did not have much confidence in the value of his conventional side. He quickly listed the negatives of that side:

Negative Expressions of Conventional

Conventional
(Negative, Extreme Expressions)
-

shortsighted
rule-follower
petty
conformist
limited
uncreative
stick-in-the-mud
do what everyone expects
lost in the crowd

Positives of John's Disliked Side

Listing the positive aspects of being conventional proved more difficult for John. He imagined what would happen if he had a conventional worker on his team who acted in a mature, constructive way. What benefits could such a person bring to a project? John eventually decided that the individual would have these characteristics:

Positive Expressions of Conventional

patient
detail-oriented
reliable
clear about expectations of others that need to be met
gets things done
knows the rules
safe
good sense of boundaries and what could rub people wrong
+
(Positive, Mature Expressions)
Conventional

John's Choice of a High Performance Oxymoron

John then looked over the lists of positives, picking the one that was most descriptive of him at his best:

» At his best as a conventional person, John is reliable.

» When at his best as an extrovert, John is an excellent communicator.

Thus, when he is at his best, John is a "reliable communicator." That is his High Performance Oxymoron. At these times John is someone you can count on. He communicates to others in ways they can understand, and they sense he can be trusted.

John's Choice of a Nightmare Oxymoron

Similarly, John looked over the list of negatives, picking the one from each side that was most descriptive of him at his worst:

» When he is at his worst as a conventional person, he is shortsighted, a petty rule follower.

» At his worst as an extrovert, he is a windbag, always talking, dominating others.

At his worst, John decided that he is a "shortsighted windbag." That is his Nightmare Oxymoron.

John's Perception-Shifting Diagram

The complete Perception-Shifting diagram graphically displays the most positive and negative expressions of John's core personal paradox. John's Original Oxymoron, "conventional extrovert," is shown at the center of the diagram:

John's Perception-Shifting Diagram

Reliable Communicator
High Performance Oxymoron

patient	
detail-oriented	
reliable	enthused by outside world
clear about expectations	friendly
others need to meet	open
gets things done	*good communicator*
knows the rules	energetic
safe	fun
good sense of boundaries and	good humored
what could rub people wrong	good listener
+	**+**
Conventional Original Oxymoron	**Extrovert**
–	**–**
shortsighted	always talking
rule-follower	always center stage
petty	dominating others
conformist	preaching
limited	*windbag*
uncreative	unconcerned
stick-in-the-mud	with others' feelings
do what everyone expects	easily interrupted
lost in the crowd	from work

Shortsighted Windbag
Nightmare Oxymoron

It's Your Turn

Now take yourself through the process of Perception-Shifting, and expand your understanding of the positive and negative expressions of your core personal paradox. Make lists of descriptors for the positive and negative expressions of each side of your core personal paradox—your oxymoron—that give an image of how you would be behaving if you were expressing each aspect. As in the John and Renee examples, you will see that even your most apparently negative characteristics have positive and constructive expressions, and indeed your most apparently positive qualities can have negative and destructive expressions.

Use the following format as a model for Perception-Shifting your personal oxymoron. Instructions are provided following the form.

High Performance Oxymoron

_____

+   +

_____ Original Oxymoron _____

–   –

Nightmare Oxymoron

To produce a perception-shifted diagram of the positive and negative expressions of each side of your core personal paradox, we've listed the parts of the process below, with instructions.

2a. List Positives of Preferred Side

List positive expressions of the side of your core personal paradox that you like best.

Write your Original Oxymoron on the lines on either side of the words "Original Oxymoron." First work with the side of your Original Oxymoron that you like best. Identify a number (at least five) of expressions of that quality that are positive and write those qualities on the lines above the original word (above the "plus" sign).

2b. List Negatives of Preferred Side

> List negative (extreme) expressions of the side of your core personal paradox that you like best.

Now identify extreme (negative) expressions of the quality. Note that these are *not* the opposites of the positive expressions, but *expressions of the extreme manifestations of the quality.* Write these words on the lines below the original word (under the "minus" sign).

2c. Negatives of Disliked Side

> List negative (extreme) expressions of the side of your core personal paradox that you like least.

Now work the other side of your Original Oxymoron. Identify negatives associated with the extreme expressions of the quality. Again, remember that these are not the opposites of the positive qualities but expressions of the extreme manifestations of the quality. Write these words on the lines below the original word.

2d. List Positives of Disliked Side

> List positive expressions of the side of your core personal paradox that you like least.

Identify at least five expressions of that quality that are positive and write those qualities on the lines above the original word. If you have difficulty finding positives of the disliked side, ask yourself, "Since I have this characteristic, what would it look like if I were to begin to express it in its positive form?" Or ask it in the third person. "If someone had this characteristic and was expressing it in some positive way, how would it show up in his or her life?"

2e. Choose a High Performance Oxymoron

> Choose a High Performance Oxymoron for yourself that captures the positive expression of both sides of your core personal paradox.

A High Performance Oxymoron is a statement of how you express both of your paradoxical qualities in their most positive, mature, and constructive way. It describes you when you are at your best. It is developed from the words and phrases in the top half of both sides of the Perception-Shifting diagram. Usually a person simply picks the two that together seem most true. However, it is also possible to continue to "play" with the words until the right ones pop up.

For example, one person's Original Oxymoron was "idealistic logician," capturing both his enthusiastic ability to see the best of what is possible in a situation, as well as his way of figuring out how to bring that about, substantiating every step with concrete logic and practicality. He experimented with several possibilities for his High Performance Oxymoron, coming up with "problem-solving romantic," "humanitarian thinker," and "practical visionary." He chose problem-solving romantic as his High Performance Oxymoron.

Choose one for yourself and put it at the top of the model page.

2f. Choose a Nightmare Oxymoron

Choose a Nightmare Oxymoron for yourself that captures the negative expression of both sides of your core personal paradox.

A Nightmare Oxymoron is a statement of how you express your core paradoxical qualities in their most negative way. It describes you when you are at your worst. It is developed from the words and phrases in the bottom half of the Perception-Shifting diagram. Choose one word or expression from each of the negative lists and combine them. Then put it at the bottom of the page. As with the High Performance Oxymoron, you can continue to "play" with the words to find the most powerful expression of your core personal paradox at its worst.

Suggestions and Caveats About Perception-Shifting

Here are some ways to avoid getting stalled.

» Depersonalize Each Aspect. It is easier to generate lists of descriptors for each side if you think in third person. For example, if "disciplined slob" is your oxymoron, typically you will have trouble seeing the positives of "slob." If you think of *someone else* who could accurately be described as a slob, but it seems to work positively, you will get much further. If that person gets away with being a slob, but also seems successful because of it, he or she is a good example to help you understand what the positive expression of "slob" looks like.

With this distancing of yourself from the word, you can usually see the positives; in this case, that the very *lack of concern for social convention* of a slob can be a strength when a team has to resist pressure to conform. Such a person is simply *indifferent to such pressure* and at his or her best can encourage everyone to resist.

» Recognize that Some Words Are Already Negative. Some original Oxymorons turn out ultimately to be the person's nightmare, and they will eventually be placed at the bottom on the person's Perception-Shifting diagram. "Obsessive slob" might be such an example. The Perception-Shifting process involves asking, "What is the more positive trait that 'slob' is really the negative expression of?" This leads to the notion that the mid-point might be "disorganized," and that the top of the diagram might be "indifference to social convention" or "unflappable under pressure to conform." Similarly, the more positive expression of "obsessive" might be "hard-driving," and the top of the diagram might be "focused."

The complete Perception-Shifting Diagram might look like this:

Focused Pressure Resister
High Performance Oxymoron

pressure resister	committed
relaxed	*focused*
unflappable under	high energy
pressure to conform	unstoppable
steady	pushing forward
secure	urgent
individual thinker	hustling
self-confident	steer the course
	accelerates the pace

+		+
Driven	Original Oxymoron	**Indifferent**
–		–

attacking	disorderly
obsessive	chaotic
hasty	slacker
compulsive	indifferent
myopic	careless
repulsive	mediocre
fanatical	*slob*
	unconcerned
	lack of attention

Obsessive Slob
Nightmare Oxymoron

» Find the Extremes, Not the Opposites. In Perception-Shifting, the most important rule is to find the negatives by taking each side to its extreme, rather than just listing its opposite. For example, let's say that the initial oxymoron is "happy-go-lucky shark." To find the negatives of "happy-go-lucky," take it to its extreme. Imagine a person who is *so* happy-go-lucky that she is ineffective and useless. What does it look like if your happy-go-lucky trait is out of control, rather than being something you know how to use positively? Using this method, the negatives of happy-go-lucky" are "off-the-wall," "irresponsible," "untrustworthy," and so forth. The negatives are *not* the opposites, such as "driven" and "focused."

Similarly, the way to find the negatives of "shark" is to take it to its extreme. Imagine someone who is so shark-like that the effect is dangerous and destructive. What happens when shark-like tendencies begin to run out of control, rather than being something the person can use in a controlled way to achieve results? Using this method, the negatives of "shark" are "attacking everything," "unpredictable," "destructive," "in it only for himself." The negatives of "shark" are *not* its opposites, such as "gentle" and "cooperative."

» Test for Personal Truth. When you have used Perception-Shifting on your oxymoron, you should be able to recall examples in your life when you expressed each of the qualities you have listed. You should be able to relate a real life story for each of the four quadrants. If you can't, chances are the Perception-Shifting has not been thoroughly performed. It needs more work.

In the end, you should recognize yourself in both the nightmare and the high performance manifestations.

Oxymorons in Action Produce Positive Behavior

Since expressing contradictory qualities and finding their mature, positive expression leads directly to a person's best work, no one should want to be one-sided. In fact, it is to the particular advantage of those involved in business relationships (e.g., manager-employee, salesperson-customer), as well as personal relationships (e.g., parent-child, husband-wife), to become sensitive to the paradoxical qualities in people and endeavor to bring those traits out positively.

As a rule, no one can sustain a high level of performance for an extended period of time using only one side of his or her paradoxical nature.

We turn now to how to apply Paradoxical Thinking to improving your performance. Chapter 4 focuses on defining a problem or goal for yourself. Chapter 5 shows how to achieve that goal in a fresh way.

SUMMARY OF KEY POINTS

✓ Every characteristic embodies potentially good and bad, positive and negative, and mature and immature aspects.

✓ Eliminating an inherent aspect of our nature is extremely difficult, and usually not wise.

✓ Rather than trying to suppress an inherent negative characteristic, learn how to use the characteristic in positive, mature, and constructive ways.

✓ "Perception-Shifting" expands the potential uses of your characteristics by helping you understand all of their positive and negative possibilities.

✓ The steps in the Perception-Shifting process are

    2a. List positives of preferred side

    2b. List negatives of preferred side

    2c. List negatives of disliked side

    2d. List positives of disliked side

    2e. Choose a High Performance Oxymoron

    2f. Choose a Nightmare Oxymoron

✓ When Perception-Shifting, remember to

    » Depersonalize each aspect

    » Recognize that some words are already negative

    » Look for extremes, not opposites

    » Test for personal truth

4

Defining Your Problem Situation and Setting Your Goal

[Reported exchange between two U.S. warships during the Pacific campaign in World War II.]

One ship's navigational equipment had failed and it had been circling aimlessly for a number of days. When it spotted another US warship, it radioed, "Where are we?"

The new warship replied, "Where are you headed?"

The lost ship replied, "We don't know."

To which the new ship replied, "If you don't know where you're going, it doesn't make much difference where you are."

> — Told as a joke by Admiral Rickover at the
> beginning of a speech heard by one of the
> authors

The next step—Step 3 of the five-step Paradoxical Thinking process—is to define the problem you want to apply it to and set a goal for yourself. The point of this step is to structure the way the problem is defined and the goal is set so that Paradoxical Thinking will work.

This step has four parts:

Step 3. Defining Your Problem Situation and Setting Your Goal

3a. Describe your unsatisfactory choices

3b. Explain the situation's effects on you

3c. Assess your past efforts

3d. Write a goal statement with a deadline

Volumes have been written about goal setting, and we believe there are many ways to set goals, most of which are valuable. What we highlight here, and illustrate with Renee and John, are the factors that are necessary for Paradoxical Thinking to work and some related aspects that come up regularly when clients apply Paradoxical Thinking to real situations.

Pick an Important, Current Problem or Goal

At this point, probably the most powerful thing you can do to maximize the value you can get from this book is to pick an important, current problem in your life and use it as the focus for working through the Paradoxical Thinking steps.

With any new idea, you typically will go through several phases while integrating it into your personal kit of useful tools. The "importance factor" (how important it is to you to solve your problem) provides the motivation to get through the sometimes difficult learning curve associated with mastering it. A meaningful application ensures that you will learn what aspects of the tool have potential for you, what uses of the tool you probably don't need, and what areas need to be customized.

Thus we recommend that you commit to using Paradoxical Thinking with something that is important enough to demand your attention and to be worthy of your effort, such as a situation in which you have a significant stake in the outcome and need a different way of approaching it, or your loss could be substantial. Only this way can you master the tool and test its personal usefulness.

Here are a variety of situations in which Paradoxical Thinking has been useful to some of our clients. You might be facing something similar and be stimulated by these suggestions. However, these are by no means the only types of situations in which Paradoxical Thinking can generate insight.

1. A particular project that is behind schedule or has other difficulties, such as:
   » Closing a sale that will make or break your results for the year
   » Being accountable for a 20 percent reduction in costs over the calendar year and now that it is September, you have achieved only an 8 percent reduction
   » Getting your house sold at a fair price now that your offer on a new house has been accepted

2. A difficult emotional issue, whether personal or work-related, such as:
   » Dealing with a boss who is taking credit for your ideas and work
   » Working out child visitation rights in a divorce settlement
   » Being ordered to do something that seems unethical

3. A critical decision that will have a major effect on your life or someone else's, such as:
   » Caring for an aging parent who wants to continue to live at home when the need for extended care is increasing
   » Making an important career decision during a transitional time of your life
   » Deciding whether to take a job offer in another state when your family is happy where you are now

4. An important client relationship that is going nowhere, such as:
   » A particular client to whom you have been trying to sell, but nothing you do seems to move the sale along
   » A client who was not treated well by your predecessor and is taking it out on you

5. A particularly difficult relationship that is frustrating, draining your energy, and reducing your overall results, such as:

> » Being caught in the middle of an escalating feud between two sides of your family

> » Trying to work out a cooperative marketing effort with a competitor who seems to take advantage of your efforts

> » Dealing with a relative who is staying with you, hasn't been able to find a job, and is living off of your income

We have found that people can creatively apply Paradoxical Thinking to almost any problem or opportunity, though it is particularly valuable in ones where the only apparent alternatives are uniformly bad.

3a. Describe Your Unsatisfactory Choices

The best way to characterize a situation so that you can use Paradoxical Thinking is to state the unsatisfactory choices among which you seem to have to choose. A truthful, up-front assessment of the apparent choices available sets the entire process for applying Paradoxical Thinking off to a good start.

Within each of the problem situations listed above, there appears to be a choice between two unsatisfactory alternatives, neither one of which will have a particularly positive impact on the situation. To take just three of them as examples, the different alternatives could be characterized as choices between

> » Keeping quiet and letting your boss take credit for your ideas and work (while you privately fume), going along with what you believe is wrong—or—confronting the boss and risking getting fired

> » Confronting a relative who is living off you about getting a job, and risking the wrath of the rest of the family—or—letting the relative freeload and privately biting your tongue

> » Taking the lateral transfer offered by your company when your office was closed, which means moving to a new city—or—staying in your city where your family is happy and looking for a job with a new company

Neither of the two choices as characterized is a good one.

An *"either/or" mindset when neither is satisfactory means you need a conceptual breakthrough.* A particularly good time to apply Paradoxical Thinking is when you feel that you must make a choice between two unsatisfactory alternatives (classically called a "lesser of two evils" choice). The process generates unusual viewpoints, a broader-based understanding of the true nature of the problem, and a pathway toward a more satisfying, high performance resolution.

3b. Explain the Situation's Effects on You

When you are struggling with an activity, it is often hard to see clearly why you seem to be stuck. Often your goal is initially stated as a wish that the external world would change. To take our two illustrative examples, Renee wished the bank would change and give her access to higher level positions. John wanted Arthur to change, to act differently and more responsibly.

There is nothing wrong with trying to bring about the change that you want. But as long as the cause of the problem is defined as something exclusively external to yourself, you will tend to think politically or manipulatively: What tactic can I take here? What can I say to this person or that person to get the result I want? It is often these tactical and manipulative behaviors that aren't working. A mother tries to manipulate her teenager by threats or bribes, but it doesn't work. A manager gives false praise to a problem employee in the hopes that the person's behavior will get better. Usually the manipulator doesn't understand the situation fully enough to know what will work, and the particular tactics seem phony and affect others in negative ways.

Paradoxical Thinking involves consciously looking at yourself first, assessing your own behavior honestly, and then bringing both sides of yourself fully to bear on the problem situation. Rather than starting out thinking externally, first put yourself into your paradoxical and ultimately high performance mode. Out of that will flow actions that will have the effect of changing the external world in the way you want.

To get into your own paradoxical mode, goal setting requires a personal connection to what makes the situation a problem for you. Don't initially jump to a description of what's wrong in the situation that needs changing. Instead, describe in personal terms how the situation is affecting you. How is it affecting you that your teenage son is on drugs, or that your boss is taking credit for your work, or that your relative is freeloading off you, or that your competitors say they want to have an alliance but seem to be taking advantage of you at every opportunity?

An examination of how the situation is affecting you often reveals deep personal values that are important in any goal statement and also deeply held self-images that may or may not be appropriate. In particular, if you are holding an image of yourself that is inappropriate (e.g., Renee's concern about how it would look to her MBA colleagues if she left a high level bank position to start a flower business), it may get in the way of your willingness to really pursue what you want and think is right.

3c. Assess Your Past Efforts

Detailed descriptions of what has been tried so far and your reasoning for why you thought your actions would work are invaluable. The list of what hasn't worked reveals the current field of play. Your reasoning helps to reveal limitations in your thinking about the situation. Obviously, if you thought something would work, tried it, and found that it didn't, your understanding of the situation is in some way incomplete or even wrong.

Paradoxical Thinking has the power to uncover ways of viewing a situation that are quite new and different. We have found it valuable for people to have documented their past unsuccessful strategies so that they don't fall back into their old ways of justifying actions that won't work. Then they are open to the new ideas suggested by Paradoxical Thinking.

3d. Write a Goal Statement with a Deadline

We like the definition of a goal as "a dream with a deadline." Good goal statements should include as much as possible of what the ideal outcome is, complete with objective indicators of success.

We also like writing goal statements as a completion of the sentence stem:

I'm going to find a way to . . . (change something for the better) . . . *by* . . . (date) . . .

This mentally suggests to people to be open-minded about *how* they will achieve the goal.

The statement should include how the situation is to change:

from . . . (whatever the current situation is, as described by the success indicators)

to . . . (whatever the goal statement is, as described by the indicators).

The goal statement should also include a time by when it needs to have happened.

Goal statements need to be as complete and as carefully constructed as possible. We like the caution

Be careful what you wish for—it might come true.

Here are a few goal statements from some recent cases:

A computer salesman frustrated with his inability to make more than isolated sales to a company we call Ajax Corp. wrote this statement:

I'm going to find a way to win the [Ajax Corp.] contract to link its manufacturing operation to its retail outlet sales, using [my company's] products. I will go *from* making isolated sales of some hardware and software *to* single supplier status for the whole system in the next three months.

An internal corporate consultant working with a critical management team wrote this goal:

I'm going to find a way to help Fred and his team decide on a set of priorities for their work that optimizes the results the whole team can achieve. The team will go *from* each person separately maneuvering to increase his departmental interests *to* a collective set of priorities. This will happen in the next ten weeks, in time to meet the corporate timeline for the submission of plans.

An entrepreneur attempting to raise money for an expansion wrote this goal:

I'm going to find a way to interest new investors in our European expansion so that we go *from* knocking on doors to find mildly interested investors *to* receiving several inquiries a day by the end of next quarter.

We will illustrate with Renee and John some of the additional depth that they reached when they put together an accurate definition of their problems and their goals.

Renee as an Example

Renee Described Her Unsatisfactory Choices

Renee's initial statement of her goal was that she wanted to be able to make a clear choice between staying at the bank or leaving and starting a floral design business. She either wanted to stay and feel good about it or leave and know that leaving was right for her. She did not want to remain in limbo.

When we asked her to formulate it in "either/or" terms, she was able to flesh out the nature of the choice. She described her choice as one of the following:

» Staying at the bank, with its prestige, a high salary, and a steady pay-check, but doing work that was becoming repetitive and less satis-fying;

—or—

» Leaving to start her own flower business, which was inherently risky, had no inherent prestige, and in which she had no particular expe-rience. It would likely cost her money initially as it would take awhile for the business to become profitable enough for her to even take a salary. It would be, however, emotionally satisfying (helping add beauty to special occasions) and aesthetically satisfying (she loved flowers and flower arranging), and it would force her to learn something new (retail sales).

This "forced choice" description of Renee's problem added much, but we thought there was more to be learned about how each connected to Renee's deeper values and desires.

Renee Explained How This Problem Situation Affected Her Personally

To uncover deeper motivations, we asked Renee how the current situ-ation affected or was a problem for her personally. What were the *per-sonal ways* in which it got to her?

After considerable discussion, she realized that she didn't see a future for herself in the bank that was exciting and demanded that she grow in her capabilities. She could not see a route to promotion that seemed likely; she could see little more than continuing her present activities into the future.

We asked for other ways the current situation affected her. We found there was a personal side. The travel demands and the intensity of the work made having a personal life outside of work very difficult. She saw no future personal life for herself if she stayed, and she wanted one. She sensed that if she stayed, she would simply be exploited for her knowledge, skill, and willingness to work hard.

In addition, while mergers and acquisitions were valuable, they didn't have the beauty and the artistic connection that she felt in her work with flowers. Her current job situation was depressing to her for it cut her off from the art and beauty values she deeply embraced.

Finally, she had a personal image of success that she believed needed to be met. It was in conflict with leaving the bank. In her mind, to leave was to throw away a lot of the pain and sacrifice that had gone into getting her MBA. She had raised the money to go to graduate school herself. Staying in a job that was important, demanding, prestigious, and well paid, even if it had no apparent room for future development at this time, seemed like a small price to pay. Bailing out and starting a small flower business seemed like "copping out" on herself.

She then made a summary list from this discussion of the personal elements that needed to be included in a solution. They were as follows:

» There had to be an exciting future that demanded she grow in her capabilities.

» There had to be time for a personal life or less travel if the hours were long.

» The work itself needed to have a strong element of aesthetic beauty.

» The job had to seem worthy of her effort to secure an MBA.

Once we determined the personal elements that were involved in Renee's decision, we could then use them as specific criteria to test alternatives.

Applying the Criteria to the Flower Business We first applied them to the choice of starting her own business:

» Could the flower business provide an exciting future leading to personal growth?

Renee answered that the floral business might not have a future either, in the sense that she might not be successful, but the very uncertainty of its future was exciting to her. Starting it would provide an opportunity, and then it would be up to her to create a future for herself.

» Would it allow time for a personal life?

The absence of travel would make a personal life possible, even if being an entrepreneur meant 60–80 hour weeks in the start-up phase and a personal life would have to be sandwiched into the remaining hours.

» Would it meet her need for aesthetic beauty?

This is what attracted her to the business in the first place. Flowers and floral arrangements were beautiful, and enhancing weddings, funerals, and meetings with flowers meant she added an aesthetic element to lots of people's lives.

» Could it be made worthy of her MBA?

As she thought about it, she decided she would not regard starting her own business as throwing away her MBA. If she could develop a realistic vision of what she wanted to create and then go do it, it would be fine. There was a lot of excitement and support for being an entrepreneur among her business school classmates. They would not look down on her if she created a successful business and made decent money.

Applying the Criteria to the Bank To test whether she really understood the deep personal values that were involved, she applied the same criteria to staying at the bank:

» Could the bank provide an exciting future leading to personal growth?

We asked Renee if she could find a different job in the bank that provided an opening for her to create a future for herself. She said that she might. How about a different bank? Again, her response was that that would be acceptable.

» Would it allow time for a personal life?

She replied that it would have to require less travel.

» Would it meet her need for aesthetic beauty?

She was hard pressed to come up with an area in the bank that she cared about and that had an artistic aspect to it.

» Could it be made worthy of her MBA?

It already was.

Her answers supported the criteria for an acceptable solution that she had identified.

Money We also asked her how important money was by inquiring, "What if she found a different job in the bank (or a different bank) that she cared about, with a future that she could create, with an artistic element, and no travel, *but less pay?*" Would she be interested? She said yes. Obviously there were limits to the pay cut she would be willing to take, but she was willing to accept less pay right now for a chance to do such a job if it had the possibility of a future. Did she have a sense of the level of pay the flower business would generate? Not precisely, but half her current salary would be fine. This gave her some parameters.

As a general rule *it is essential for the person to describe the problem in personal terms. Once the underlying wants and desires of the person are determined, all the facts can be brought back into the picture from a different perspective.*

Now the two choices, *plus lots of other possible solutions*, can be tested. An acceptable solution is independent of the particular choices the person has considered.

Renee Assessed Her Past Efforts

Renee briefly described the steps she had undertaken that hadn't worked in resolving this problem. Here is what she described.

Improving Her Situation at the Bank Renee had not made much of an effort to make things better at the bank. She had told her boss that she wanted more responsibility, and he had agreed he would give it to her if there was a chance, though mostly he headed the merger and acquisition teams and wouldn't likely let her head one. She had thought about specializing in a particular kind of merger or acquisition, though she hadn't pursued it. There were so few, the bank didn't need specialists.

She had not made any effort to move to another part of the bank, as horizontal moves were difficult to make. Like it or not, she was now a specialist in mergers and acquisitions. She hadn't considered taking a downward step in salary to get involved in another part of the bank. It seemed to her to violate everything she had ever heard about how to make successful career moves, particularly as a female. She had not even considered jumping to a different bank.

In general, she recognized that she had not been taking a serious look at rejuvenating her career in the bank. The discussion about money had opened this possibility somewhat, but she was skeptical of a lateral and downward move as good for her.

Investigating the Flower Business On the flower business front, she had made a number of analyses. She had developed a spreadsheet matrix on flowers and costs to help her make bids and then maintain profit margins while substituting flowers. She had produced pro forma financials and had developed a pretty good marketing plan. She was busy enough with providing flowers for friends' special occasions on weekends to be encouraged about the possibilities.

She had looked at four storefronts, though each of them met only about half of the attributes on her list of criteria. She came to the conclusion it was wiser to run the business out of her house for some time; looking for storefront space was premature. She had researched the laws and tax requirements regarding hiring employees. She had discussed possible changes in her liability insurance with her insurance company.

This process of recalling what she had done served to remind her that she had already committed a certain amount of effort, energy, and worry to this dilemma, encouraged her by helping her see what she *had* accomplished, and identified what had not been resolved. The rather perfunctory way she had attempted to improve things at the bank surprised her. She realized that she hadn't done anything that she really expected would work. It was almost as if she had decided to leave but couldn't bring herself to do it.

Her review made it clear to her that her efforts to improve things at the bank had not worked because she had not tried to achieve a particular outcome. Not being clear that she wanted to even consider staying at the bank, she had not asked for a particular kind of job or responsibility, nor enlisted the help of her boss in arranging for a lateral transfer. She had not canvassed the bank for jobs that would allow a more artistic perspective. And she had not contacted any headhunters, nor had she used her contacts with other banks to explore positions that met her criteria.

On the flower side, while she had enjoyed her weekend forays into helping her friends and made more than a little incidental income, she didn't know what it was like to run a retail business and deal with the general public instead of friends. She had not worked for or befriended people who ran other florist operations. She had not done a market survey, nor investigated the strengths and weaknesses of those who would be her direct competitors. She hadn't considered trying to buy an already established business.

Almost certainly her income would take a hit, at least initially, though she hadn't really done a hard capitalization analysis to see how much money she would need. When she made the list, she realized why she hadn't actually left the bank. There were too many factors she hadn't yet investigated.

Renee's Complete, Measurable Goal Statement with a Deadline

Stating the objective positive outcome she would like without implying a specific solution was her next task. To begin, she used the sentence stem and then wrote her desired outcomes:

I'm going to find a way to create a position for myself that will move me *from* my current position *to* one that

» has a future,

» will demand that I grow and develop,

» allows for a healthier balance between my personal and professional life,

» will bring an artistic element into my life,

» is personally satisfying and meaningful to those I care about.

She gave herself no more than six months to create a situation that met these criteria.

At this point, not determining the specific steps to accomplish the goal left the door open for an innovative approach and a fresh new idea or two for resolving the problem.

By the time Renee finished responding to the four parts of Step 3, she was clearly ready to apply her High Performance Oxymoron to achieving her goal. The exercise had served to remind Renee why it was worthwhile to take up the struggle of making a decision once again.

We will continue with that application in the next chapter.

John as an Example

With a strong background in accounting, marketing, and personnel development, and as an experienced manager who directed a staff of twenty, John understood the requirements of his company's bureaucracy as well as his customers' needs and was respected by his superiors and staff as an excellent manager. His frustration with Arthur was palpable.

John Described His Unsatisfactory Choices

John's formulation of his frustration with Arthur in "either/or" terms allowed him to more fully describe the nature of the choices he faced. He characterized the problem as:

» Either I can continue to give Arthur the level of complex responsibilities he is supposed to handle at his salary and job level, allow his intelligence, energy and enthusiasm to be engaged, and continue to have to clean up after him when he irresponsibly exceeds the limits I have set on his authority;

—or—

» I can sit on him hard, monitor him closely, clobber him when he fails to follow instructions, and get acceptable work out of him, but without engaging his intelligence, enthusiasm, or energy, and draining mine.

Both choices were unsatisfactory to John. In the former, Arthur would probably end up getting fired when he did something particularly irresponsible. At a minimum he would never really learn how to control his enthusiasm and intellect to have a valuable career in the company. In the latter, Arthur would probably leave after awhile. They both required a lot of management energy.

John had been around long enough to know that firing someone rarely was the right solution. It was expensive and time consuming to start over with a new search and hire process. He also, in another way, liked Arthur. He had voted to hire him. He knew the strengths that were there. He didn't want to lose them or see them go undeveloped. Yet John was extremely frustrated and tired of the problem of dealing with Arthur.

John Explained How This Problem Situation Affected Him Personally

John's initial personalized answers were bitter. He said that he "wanted the problems with Arthur out of his life." He wanted resolution one way or the other. As with most people, he started by recounting ways he wanted Arthur to change. He wanted Arthur to listen to his direct instructions and then to follow them. He was willing to encourage creativity, he said angrily, but not when it made the results useless.

We reiterated that while it was important to describe the changes he wanted in Arthur, Paradoxical Thinking starts with how John could change his own actions to get what *he* wanted: *John had to change how he was working with Arthur, rather than trying to change Arthur directly.* Then he might be successful in getting Arthur to change. Thus, he needed to define the problem in terms of how it affected him and what outcomes he wanted for himself. Changes in Arthur's behavior would be part of what happened, but he couldn't get there and shouldn't start by deciding how Arthur should be different.

After further discussion, John focused on the amount of time he had to take with Arthur compared to any of his other staff. It was disproportionate in relation to the payoff.

He also found Arthur's emotional volatility drained him. He didn't mind someone disagreeing with him. In fact, as any of his employees could attest, he welcomed dissent. What he found intolerable was Arthur's high-handed, arrogant disregard for procedures. Arthur seemed to regard John's instructions as authoritarian dictates of someone old and out of touch rather than sensible requirements developed out of years of experience.

In sum, he wanted the amount of time he spent with (or "on") Arthur to be appropriate for the amount of positive benefit he was receiving—not excessive because he had to correct Arthur's mistakes. And he wanted to be energized by his interactions with Arthur, not drained.

John wrote these two personal elements down as criteria:

» Time spent with Arthur should reflect the amount of positive benefit received.

» Interactions with Arthur needed to be energizing, not draining.

John immediately saw that he didn't really want Arthur to just listen and follow directions. That wouldn't be satisfying for either of them. It had been merely an initial angry response on John's part, a short-term relief response, not a real solution. With these two criteria, the problem was now defined correctly.

John Assessed His Past Efforts

John indicated that Arthur had been selected after an extensive search. He was one of the highest ranking graduates in accounting and finance from a major business school and a brilliant computer whiz.

John described what he had tried so far and what had happened. Initially John had started by giving Arthur time to get up to speed on the new accounting system, making certain that Arthur was trained carefully. Even then, there had been problems. Arthur avoided learning the system the way it was designed. He continued to resist aspects of it or belittled the design. Several times he suggested changes, which John stopped. While an occasional criticism was justified, for the most part John felt Arthur didn't know enough about the business to understand why it was designed the way it was. John had to insist Arthur spend the time and learn the system as it was, while patiently answering his questions and indicating why he was wrong in much of his criticism.

Once he was convinced Arthur understood the system, John gave him full responsibility to install the system and train the staff in the regional offices. He felt his instructions were quite clear, and Arthur hadn't followed them. In fact, Arthur had gone way beyond his authority in changing the system and had botched the installation.

When John found out what Arthur had done, he blew his stack. He angrily confronted Arthur and was dumbfounded and further annoyed when Arthur tried to defend his actions. After the confrontation, Arthur made snide comments to other employees about John's reaction, left for the day, and only the next day came in to apologize.

John found himself bouncing back and forth between believing that Arthur could be trusted to do a responsible job on his own and believing that the only way to manage Arthur was to check every detail of his work and threaten him with the wrath of the universe if he deviated from instructions.

John admitted that so far he hadn't found a successful and satisfying way to relate to Arthur. Trusting him gave him too much rope, and monitoring him just exacerbated his volatility, as well as drained John's time and energy.

What other options had he considered? For example, how about having Arthur work with the design team for a week or two? Were there horizontal moves that might get Arthur into a design job? Was Arthur too quick and knowledgeable to be good at the job of training others? John admitted he wasn't paying much attention to where Arthur might be valuable. He was trying to get Arthur to do his current job well.

In general, a careful review of what has been tried often uncovers a variety of options that haven't been considered and a preponderance of effort skewed toward a certain outcome.

John clearly had not yet produced a happy, motivated worker. Arthur seemed sullen at the prospect of redoing all the work he had done at the regional offices. While Arthur chafed at the notion that John needed to carefully review his work and provide close oversight, John was very reluctant to give Arthur any freedom until he felt Arthur's maturity and judgment warranted it. Yet John could see that Arthur's tremendous energy and vitality were not engaged.

John's Complete, Measurable Goal Statement with a Deadline

John said he would like to feel certain that when Arthur was given a responsible assignment, Arthur's tremendous energy would be engaged. In addition, he wanted Arthur to exhibit mature judgment. He wanted Arthur to understand and accomplish what had to be done, while coming to him for answers to questions that were outside his charge. He would also like Arthur to bring to him proposals that meant major changes in the parameters of his work, rather than cavalierly implementing them.

Combining these with his personal factors, John started with this sentence stem, and wrote his desired outcomes:

I'm going to find a way to move from my current frustration and dissatisfaction with Arthur to

» feeling certain that Arthur's assignments will be done accurately and well,

» engaging Arthur's tremendous energy and drive, while increasing the maturity of his judgment,

» opening the door to energizing input from Arthur, while making sure Arthur knows for what he has to get approval,

» reducing my time demands to monitor, oversee, and correct Arthur's work.

How John used Paradoxical Thinking to generate new insights about how to deal with his most difficult employee and resolve his quandary continues in chapter 5.

This chapter presents just a few of the situations to which people have applied Paradoxical Thinking. Drawing from your own life, you will likely find many more.

You Try It

To get the full benefit of the process, it is most helpful for you to pick a meaningful current activity or relationship that quickly is becoming, or has already become, a "choice problem"—you feel you have to make a choice and neither choice is satisfactory. The best situations to pick are ones that are immediate, concrete, and currently active, where a fresh insight alone could make a significant difference in results. Then work through the four key parts of this step.

3a. Describe Your Unsatisfactory Choices

Describe the problem situation in terms of its unsatisfactory choices, as you currently see them.

Characterize your problem in terms of the unsatisfactory choices that presently seem to be your only alternatives. Ask yourself, "If I were to describe my choices in this problem situation as an "either/or," how would I describe them? Try completing this sentence stem, "Either I can do . . . (and be hit by certain consequences that I don't like), or I can do . . . (and equally be hit by certain other consequences that I don't like). After you think about it for awhile, you can usually formulate the unsatisfactory alternatives. You also may have more than two. Just add additional "or" phrases.

3b. Explain the Situation's Effects on You

Explain how this problem situation affects you personally.

Try first to list all of the ways in which the problem situation is affecting you. List anything from loss of sleep to anger to negative or retaliatory behavior patterns. Each of the items on your list then becomes the germ of the deep, personal criteria which a solution must meet. Particularly avoid listing all sorts of ways in which other people or outside situations have to change for you to be happy. List how you want to be behaving and reacting.

3c. Assess Your Past Efforts

Describe what you have tried so far and what happened.

List the actions you have taken in your efforts to fix the situation. Don't let yourself get too caught up in them. Think about other alternatives. Try to figure a way to meet the criteria from 3b in some totally different way.

Reconsider any actions you are certain are right and ought to work, but they haven't. Many times people are sure they know what is wrong. However, when they act to correct a situation, it gets worse. Then they redouble their efforts, and the situation gets even worse. Parents think, for example, that their teenagers need to be disciplined, so they crack down. The teenager gets more defiant. The parents crack down harder. The teenager gets worse. If you are in a closed-loop, downward spiral like this, reconsider your initial position that cracking down is the right thing to do.

If those involved begin to realize that the problem isn't formulated correctly, and the path they are taking isn't working, they can be open to new alternatives. The parents may find that what they need to do is to really listen to their teenager. The teenager may find that he or she really needs some constraints.

Many times when we start this process, we find people still cling to their beliefs that what they did *should* have worked. It takes repeated reminders that it *didn't* work before they are willing to look at doing something very different. Just keep asking yourself honestly, "Is it working?" If the answer is no, reconsider. Move on. Don't redouble your efforts.

3d. Write a Goal Statement

Write a complete, measurable goal statement with a deadline.

Once you have sorted out the failed efforts you have made, and listed the personal reasons why the situation is a problem for you, state the desired outcome you want. Include the criteria from 3b that a particular solution needs to meet. Start with the sentence stem

I'm going to find a way to . . .

This allows you to list the outcomes you would like, without implying any particular way that you are going to achieve them. Ask yourself: "What are the objective positive outcomes I would like?" Try to list the criteria of a solution, without limiting yourself to a concrete solution. Use a "from . . . to . . ." formulation of how you want the situation to change. You will find in the next chapters a variety of ways to create what you want.

SUMMARY OF KEY POINTS

✓ Paradoxical Thinking generates unusual viewpoints, leading to a broader-based understanding of the true nature of a particular problem or opportunity.

✓ Paradoxical Thinking can be applied to almost any problem or opportunity.

✓ You can maximize the value of the Paradoxical Thinking process by applying it to a real, current problem or opportunity in your life in which you have a significant stake in the outcome.

✓ The four-part problem definition and goal setting process is

3a. Describe your unsatisfactory choices

3b. Explain the situation's effects on you

3c. Assess your past efforts

3d. Write a goal statement with a deadline

✓ Paradoxical Thinking is most useful when the problem is defined in terms of its unsatisfactory "either/or" choices among which you seem to have to choose.

✓ It is essential that you describe a particular problem or opportunity in terms that apply to you personally, not to someone else.

✓ A careful review of what has been tried, so far unsuccessfully, to resolve the problem situation often uncovers a variety of options that haven't been considered yet.

✓ Don't cling to a belief that the unsuccessful steps you have taken to resolve a current situation ought to have worked. If they haven't, and you seem to be in a downward spiral, a different approach is necessary.

5

Rating Yourself on Fletcher's Pendulum

The greatest discovery of my generation is that a human being can alter his life by altering his attitude of mind.
— WILLIAM JAMES

The next step—Step 4 of the five-step Paradoxical Thinking process—helps you assess how well you are using your core paradoxical qualities in addressing the problem or goal you have selected. We use what we have come to call Fletcher's Pendulum after Jerry Fletcher, originator of the Paradoxical Thinking process. He developed the pendulum as a simple tool for tracking the positive and negative expressions of core personal paradoxes. It makes manageable the challenge of keeping paradoxical forces continually operating in day-to-day activities.

As in previous chapters, we explain the process and illustrate it with Renee's and John's examples. We then elaborate on how you can use it and finally conclude the chapter with some suggestions and caveats about the step.

This step has four parts:

Step 4. Rating Yourself on Fletcher's Pendulum

4a. Set up your own personal pendulum

4b. Place your goal at the top

4c. Define the expression of each side

4d. Rate your current actions with respect to your goal

4a. Set Up Your Own Personal Pendulum

To set up your own Fletcher's Pendulum, go back to your Perception-Shifting diagram (chapter 3, step 2) and consider each side of your contradictory qualities as a scale running from +100 through zero to –100. A number of examples are given in that chapter.

Once these two scales are created, bring the two high performance points together to form an apex. Imagine now that this is a string hanging from a nail, with a weight on the bottom, and the diagram looks like a pendulum swinging back and forth between the two nightmare (–100) positions:

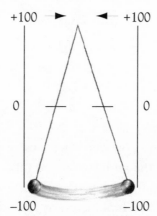

The use of a pendulum diagram reflects the experience that people describe of swinging from one side to the other when they are caught in a problem that seems to have no resolution. When people are caught in these swings, they are in their "nightmare." The swings diminish once people begin bringing both sides of their contradictory nature into play and express them maturely and responsibly. At the apex, both sides of the paradox are fully present simultaneously.

For example, Renee found herself unable to make a decision. She would swing back and forth between the choices of remaining at the bank or opening a small floral design business.

Similarly, John swung back and forth between trying to be helpful to and trusting of Arthur or angrily blowing up at him and keeping him on a tight leash.

Neither Renee nor John liked either of the alternatives they could see initially, so they vacillated, consuming lots of personal energy as they agonized over what to do.

In addition to placing the High Performance, Original, and Nightmare Oxymorons on the pendulum, add the words and phrases that elaborate both the positive and negative expressions of each side. These words come from the Perception-Shifting exercise in chapter 3.

4b. Place Your Goal at the Top

Once the pendulum is laid out, it can be used for any particular problem. Ideally, place the written description of the problem/goal at the top of the pendulum so it is clear you are applying your paradoxical characteristics to achieving it.

4c. Define the Expression of Each Side

Using the words you listed on your pendulum diagram, define how you would be acting toward your goal if you were expressing the high performance qualities of one side of your oxymoron. Do the same for the nightmare qualities of that side also. Then repeat the exercise for the opposite side of your oxymoron, describing your high performance and nightmare actions.

4d. Rating Your Current Actions with Respect to Your Goal

Taking each side of your oxymoron in turn, rate yourself on how consistent with the high performance expression of that side your current actions have been. The following example will make the rating step clearer.

Renee Rates Herself

Renee's Pendulum Setup

Renee's self-doubting side, arranged on a scale from +100 through zero to –100 looks like:

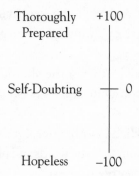

Her overachiever side can be placed on a similar scale:

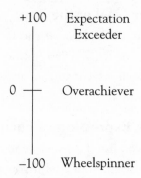

Renee put these two scales together and then added the words from her Perception-Shifting diagram.

Analysis of Renee's Pendulum With this diagram we can see in general what happens to Renee when she can't make up her mind. She starts swinging back and forth between the two sides. If she doubts herself too much, she feels hopeless and gives up entirely. The pendulum swings far to the left on the following diagram. In the current example, she resigns herself to staying in her current position at the bank and tries to convince herself to be grateful for the prestige and the steady paycheck.

This goes on for awhile, usually while anger and frustration build up. When she finally gets fed up, her overachiever side gets activated.

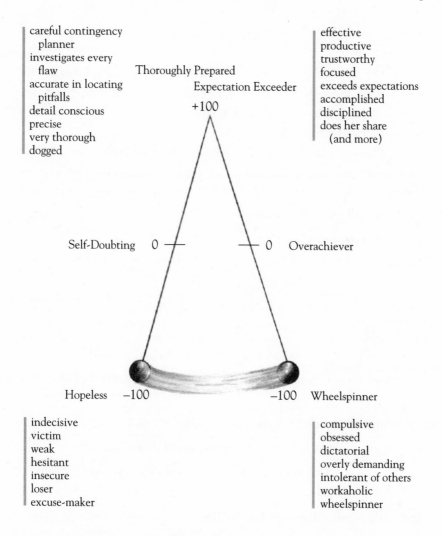

careful contingency
  planner
investigates every
  flaw
accurate in locating
  pitfalls
detail conscious
precise
very thorough
dogged

Thoroughly Prepared
    Expectation Exceeder
      +100

effective
productive
trustworthy
focused
exceeds expectations
accomplished
disciplined
does her share
  (and more)

Self-Doubting   0   0   Overachiever

Hopeless   −100   −100   Wheelspinner

indecisive
victim
weak
hesitant
insecure
loser
excuse-maker

compulsive
obsessed
dictatorial
overly demanding
intolerant of others
workaholic
wheelspinner

The pendulum begins to swing to the right on the diagram. She bursts into a frenzy of activity to resolve the problem once and for all. But since she isn't clear about what she wants, she falls into disconnected wheelspinning activities. In the current example, she looks at storefronts (though it's not clear it's wise to have one or that having one is a high priority). She investigates hiring people (though again she doesn't know whether she wants any employees). At the height of her frenzied efforts, the pendulum has swung far to the right. When she finally gets exhausted and frustrated that the problem isn't yielding, the pendulum starts to swing back to the left, and she starts to withdraw again into hopelessness.

There is probably nothing more maddening to a usually successful person than a problem that doesn't yield to overwhelming effort. Yet when the proper insight about what to do isn't present, all the effort in the world can't resolve the problem.

As Renee's responses to her dilemma about whether to stay at the bank or go into business for herself swung back and forth, they drained her energy. She simultaneously wanted the problem to go away and feared actually making a decision.

Renee's Goal Statement

Renee added her goal statement from chapter 4 to the top of the pendulum:

Find a way to create a position for myself that

» has a future,

» demands that I grow and develop,

» allows for a healthier balance between my personal and professional life,

» brings an artistic element into my life,

» is personally satisfying and meaningful to those I care about.

She gave herself no more than six months to have created a situation that met these criteria.

Renee's Definitions of Each Side

Renee looked first at her "expectation-exceeder/overachiever/wheel-spinner" side. She considered the list of words and phrases in the upper right corner and described how she would be acting toward her goal if she were using her overachiever trait in a positive way. That is, trying to create the type of job she wanted in the way an expectation-exceeder would. She decided that she would be disciplined, productive, and focused, probably following a plan or list of what needed to be accomplished to help her make the decision. For the stay-at-the-bank option, she would be looking at possible places in the bank that would give her what she wanted, inquiring about openings, asking people to recommend her, telling the people in charge what she would be able to do if they gave her the chance.

Using the list of words and phrases in the lower right corner, Renee described how she would be acting toward her goal if she were using her overachiever trait in a negative way. She would be wheel spinning; redoing work she had already done, much as a person who has misplaced something keeps looking in the same drawers for it. Or she would be scattering her effort over so many fronts that she didn't accomplish anything.

She also decided that she would be behaving in ways that were increasingly obsessive, compulsive, demanding, intolerant and displaying workaholic tendencies. In effect, she would be acting as if she knew what to do when she didn't. For the flower business option, she might be looking at many storefronts in which to open her business, all in poor locations, and driving herself ragged going over figures for her business, without really testing the figures against actual florist businesses. She might be compulsively telling prospective customers she was leaving the bank to bolster her commitment, driving up their expectations before she was ready, rather than carefully interviewing them about what they would want in a flower business if they were to come to her.

Then Renee looked at her "thoroughly prepared/self-doubting/ hopeless" side. She used the list of words and phrases in the upper left to describe how she would be acting toward her goal if she were using her self-doubting side in a positive way. She decided she would be thoroughly prepared for a variety of things that might go wrong. She'd be investigating every potential pitfall and developing contingency plans for every possibility.

Using the list of words and phrases in the lower left, Renee described how she would be acting toward her goal if she were expressing her self-doubting side in a negative way and letting it control her. She would be feeling hopeless. She would be finding so many things that might go wrong that she'd feel like a fool for even thinking she could succeed. For example, she would be convincing herself that she was terribly lucky to have the job at the bank and resolving to stay.

Renee's Self-Ratings

Renee's Overachiever Side Renee looked at which description of an overachiever best characterized how she was presently approaching making a decision to start her flower business. She decided she was in fact acting quite positively, more like an expectation exceeder.

She was preparing a business plan with a real eye to exceeding expectations, coming up with angles to outdo the competition. She was set on generating more business than she could easily handle, and she was investigating all of the aspects in a disciplined, productive way. While there were more things she wanted to do, and it was taking her longer than she thought, on the whole she felt quite good about her progress. On a scale of −100 to +100, she rated herself at +50.

On the other hand, she was not behaving nearly as well with respect to the option of staying at the bank and creating an acceptable option for herself. She hadn't been looking for an opening systematically, in a disciplined and productive way. She hadn't even engaged headhunters to see if other banks had openings. She rated her behavior toward the "stay-at-the-bank and create the position I want" option at −90.

Renee's Self-Doubting Side Renee considered which description of a self-doubter best characterized her current behavior with respect to her goal. She decided she was quite deeply into self-doubt and rated herself a −40—not terrible, but she felt so many things could go wrong that it was easier to avoid making a decision than face them. She rated herself even worse on the "stay-at-the-bank" option. She so doubted that the bank would ever allow her to do what she wanted that she hadn't even seriously asked. She rated herself at −70.

Plotting Renee's Self-Ratings on the Fletcher's Pendulum Diagram Renee plotted her responses on the Fletcher's Pendulum diagram. You can see below how she was "high-low": high on one side and low on the other with respect to starting the flower business (bold line). She was a "low-low" with respect to staying at the bank (narrow line). Her ratings of herself on both sides needed to move up higher on the pendulum to really come together.

Goal: *Find a way to* create a position for myself that

» has a future,
» demands that I grow and develop,
» allows for a healthier balance between my personal and professional life,
» brings an artistic element into my life,
» is personally satisfying and meaningful to those I care about.

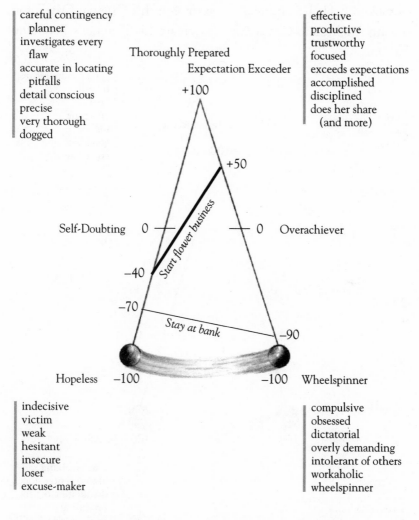

careful contingency planner	effective
investigates every flaw	productive
accurate in locating pitfalls	trustworthy
detail conscious	focused
precise	exceeds expectations
very thorough	accomplished
dogged	disciplined

Thoroughly Prepared
Expectation Exceeder
+100

+50

Self-Doubting 0 ————— 0 Overachiever

Start flower business

−40

−70

Stay at bank

−90

Hopeless −100 −100 Wheelspinner

indecisive	compulsive
victim	obsessed
weak	dictatorial
hesitant	overly demanding
insecure	intolerant of others
loser	workaholic
excuse-maker	wheelspinner

Now that Renee knew by her own self-ratings what she was doing wrong—what side of herself she needed to activate more strongly to create a high performance outcome—she needed to identify actions she could take to activate the thoroughly prepared side more fully. These would be actions that would lead her to rate herself higher on that side of the pendulum. That is the subject of the next chapter.

John Rates Himself

John's Pendulum Setup

To help resolve his dilemma with Arthur, John mapped his oxymorons—his High Performance Oxymoron, his Original Oxymoron, and his Nightmare Oxymoron—to create his Fletcher's Pendulum diagram:

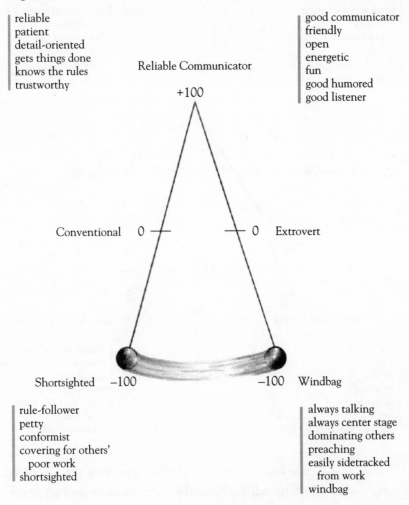

reliable
patient
detail-oriented
gets things done
knows the rules
trustworthy

good communicator
friendly
open
energetic
fun
good humored
good listener

Reliable Communicator

+100

Conventional   0 ——| |—— 0   Extrovert

Shortsighted   −100   −100   Windbag

rule-follower
petty
conformist
covering for others'
   poor work
shortsighted

always talking
always center stage
dominating others
preaching
easily sidetracked
   from work
windbag

Analysis of John's Pendulum From this diagram you can get a sense of how John's paradoxical qualities work, independent of his interaction with Arthur. When he is at his best, he is an energetic, fun, enthusiastic extrovert, a great listener and communicator, and someone who is deeply trustworthy and reliable, who knows the rules, gets things done right, and pays attention to details.

At his worst, John becomes a petty conformist, insisting on following rules, even if they are shortsighted, or his natural extrovertedness becomes preachy and dominating, with him insisting on being center stage and putting down anyone who disagrees or has an alternative idea to his own. In his nightmare he will swing back and forth between these two sides.

John's Goal Statement

John's goal statement from chapter 4 was

I'm going to find a way to

» ensure that Arthur's work is done accurately and well,

» engage Arthur's tremendous energy and drive,

» open the door to energizing input from Arthur,

» reduce the time demands to monitor, oversee, and correct Arthur's work to free me for other responsibilities.

John wrote this goal at the top of his pendulum and then made his own assessment of how he was approaching his goal of improving his working relationship with Arthur.

John's Definitions of Each Side

The words on the left side of John's personal pendulum describe the positive and negative expressions of John's "reliable/conventional/shortsighted" side. Using the words at the upper left, John described how he would be acting toward his goal if he were using his conventional tendencies in their most positive form with respect to Arthur. He decided he would be patient and reliable, acting to get things done in a way that was consistent with the rules. He would be willing to bend the rules, if necessary, to get an even better result that was consistent with the intent of the rules. He would also be detail-oriented, making sure there was no room for things to fall through the cracks.

Using the words in the lower left, John described how he would be acting toward his goal if he were using his conventional tendencies in their most negative way. He decided he would be shortsighted and petty, insisting that Arthur conform exactly to the rules and not deviate from them, even if some deviation would produce a better result. He also would be quite uninterested in anything Arthur had to say about it.

We then turned to John's "communicator/extrovert/windbag" side. Using the words and phrases on the right side of his pendulum, he described how he would be acting toward his goal if he were using his extrovert tendencies in their most positive form with respect to Arthur. He decided that would be friendly, open, and good humored toward him. If he were using his extrovert tendencies in their negative form when trying to achieve the goal, he'd be a windbag, always talking, preaching, and overruling any input from Arthur.

John's Self-Ratings

John's Conventional Side John looked at which words on the conventional side of the diagram best described how he actually was behaving with respect to Arthur. He decided he had become increasingly shortsighted, working "by the book," insisting that Arthur follow every rule. He had, in his own judgment, become a petty tyrant. When rating how bad he had become, John gave himself a –70 rating.

John's Extrovert Side In looking at which words on the extrovert side best described his behavior towards Arthur, he saw with a sense of real insight that the negative ones described him perfectly. In the past few months he had become "a preachy windbag" toward Arthur, so he gave himself a –80 rating.

Defending His Actions John also, however, presented a justification for his actions, a common reaction, even though he was not being successful. It was as if he believed that there was no other way, even in the face of the obvious failure of the tactics he'd been using. In effect, John felt that since Arthur had a tendency to break any rule and his judgment was weak, John had to act like a petty tyrant to keep Arthur from doing even more damage.

Notice the downward slide that this creates. No one should retain an employee who could only do damage if left to himself! How likely would it be that the employee would produce outstanding work?

The important thing was to get John back on track toward his stated goal. Then he needed to assess whether his current actions toward Arthur were achieving it. When asked how his current strategy was working, he said, somewhat angrily and resignedly, that it wasn't. That was why he was talking about it. He didn't like being a petty tyrant. Furthermore, he wasn't making use of Arthur's imaginative capabilities. However, he had responsibilities for the success of his unit, and he couldn't take the risk that Arthur, in trying to be creative, would do something crazy instead and leave a mess for John or the others to clean up.

How much of his energy was drained to manage Arthur so tightly? He agreed that he was terribly drained. He wasn't at his best at all. He was using up a lot of time that could be best spent on other, more rewarding activities, with more significant payoffs for the company.

There is no question that he had to manage Arthur in a way that minimized the risk to the company. However, the path that he had chosen was a self-fulfilling prophecy. Once he believed he had to manage Arthur very tightly, he was hurting himself, and there was no way for the situation to get better. Was he willing to look for an alternative way to work with Arthur, one that used his paradoxical sides in a positive way and wouldn't drain his energy? He went back to the details of his goal statement, particularly the part about having energizing interactions with Arthur. He then decided that he would like to find a better alternative.

Plotting John's Self-Ratings on His Fletcher's Pendulum Diagram
John's responses looked like this on his Fletcher's Pendulum diagram.

Goal: *I'm going to find a way to*

» ensure that Arthur's work is done accurately and well,
» engage Arthur's tremendous energy and drive,
» open the door to energizing input from Arthur,
» reduce the time demands to monitor, oversee and correct Arthur's work to free me for other responsibilities.

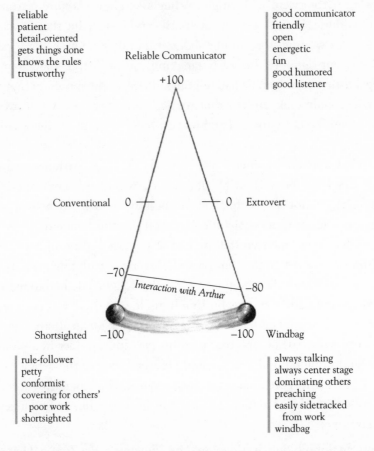

reliable
patient
detail-oriented
gets things done
knows the rules
trustworthy

Reliable Communicator
+100

good communicator
friendly
open
energetic
fun
good humored
good listener

Conventional   0   ⊢   ⊣   0   Extrovert

−70
Interaction with Arthur   −80

Shortsighted   −100   −100   Windbag

rule-follower
petty
conformist
covering for others'
     poor work
shortsighted

always talking
always center stage
dominating others
preaching
easily sidetracked
     from work
windbag

The Fletcher's Pendulum diagram showed John that he was expressing both sides of himself in their negative forms. He was swinging back and forth between self-righteously preaching to Arthur about how irresponsible and lacking in judgment he was and angrily insisting that he conform to rules. The combination of his anger and his sense of helplessness had led him to feeling that the only solution was to fire Arthur. John's feelings are typical of someone who is behaving at his worst on both sides of the pendulum and caught swinging between them.

When you are caught in this painful swing between the two sides of your contradictory nature, it is imperative to understand the dynamics of such a swing. Choose actions that will raise your ratings and move you upward on the pendulum and into the mature expression of your contradictory nature.

That is the subject of the next chapter.

_____

It's Your Turn

4a. Set Up Your Own Personal Pendulum

Now set up your own personal pendulum diagram. Take your three oxymorons from Chapter 3, along with the other words that add definition to them and arrange them with the

High Performance Oxymoron (HPO) on the top,

Original Oxymoron (OO) in the middle, and

Nightmare Oxymoron (NO) at the bottom.

Write a "+100" at the apex and "–100" at the swinging ends. We suggest you read the "suggestions and caveats" section at the end of this chapter before doing this step.

4b. Place Your Goal at the Top

Next, formulate a simple statement of your problem situation or decision that you want to resolve, using your goal statement from chapter 4. Put it above the apex of the pendulum. For the process to work it must be a very real problem or goal that is currently an issue for you. The process works best if you can state the objective, positive outcome you'd like, without implying any particular solution. Example: "I'm going to find a way to reach agreement with person X about how to complete the project that satisfies us both."

4c. Define the Expression of Each Side of Your Oxymorons

Using the words that add definition to each quadrant of your diagram, describe what it would be like if you were acting toward your goal in each of the four ways. This defines your scales and allows you to make self-ratings that have real meaning to you.

4d. Rate Your Current Actions with Respect to Your Goal

Finally, rate your current actions with respect to resolving the problem or achieving your goal. Have you been in your nightmare space, swinging back and forth between two alternatives, neither of which seems to work? Or, are you high on one side and low on the other? In either case, ask yourself what actions you would have to take to raise your self-ratings to be positive on both sides, and then determine to what degree you are taking those actions.

Suggestions and Caveats for Setting Up Your Pendulum

You May Have to Reverse the Order of One or Two of Your Oxymorons

When setting up your Fletcher's Pendulum, you must be careful to put the words related to one side of your oxymoron on the same side of the pendulum. Each side must represent a scale from +100 to –100. Sometimes achieving this means reversing the order of the words in an oxymoron (and this often results in an awkward phrase).

Here are two examples that required such a reversal. Again, this may not apply to your oxymorons, but if it does, these examples will help:

» Person 1's Oxymorons. To lay out the following three oxymorons on the pendulum, one of the three had to be reversed:

How First Written	How Realigned for Placement on Pendulum
HPO: Magical Charger	Magical Charger
OO: Steamrolling Tinkerbell	*Tinkerbell Steamrolling*
NO: Unnoticeable Ruffian	Unnoticeable Ruffian

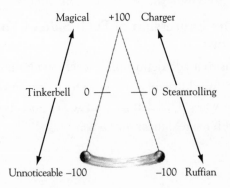

Magical   +100   Charger

Tinkerbell   0 ──┼─   ┼── 0 Steamrolling

Unnoticeable –100   –100 Ruffian

» Person 2's Oxymorons. To lay out the following three oxymorons on the pendulum, the Original and Nightmare Oxymorons had to be reversed:

How First Written	How Realigned for Placement on Pendulum
HPO: Observing Warrior	Observing Warrior
OO: Roaring Phantom	Phantom Roaring
NO: Raging Nonentity	Nonentity Raging

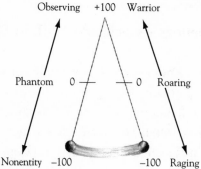

Many people become confused by ignoring this important step in the process. Realign the three oxymorons if necessary for placement on the pendulum so that each side of the pendulum is a scale running from +100 through zero to –100.

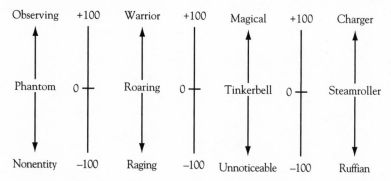

Rate Yourself

In learning to use the pendulum, it is helpful to remember that *the ratings are self-ratings.* You are in control. If you can use the contradictory sides of yourself simultaneously and positively in dealing with a problematic situation, you will do better.

The pendulum enables you to make your own judgment about how well you are currently using your paradoxical qualities as strengths. Then, you can come up with action steps to raise your self-ratings toward the apex.

If you are successful, your ratings of yourself will get better. No one else is rating you, and no one else is demanding that you behave in a certain way. The pendulum enables you to see in what way you are not using your core paradoxical qualities effectively and what to do to bring both to bear effectively on solving your problem.

Be Aware of Feelings Associated with Low Self-Ratings on the Pendulum

Over the years, it became clear to us that certain patterns of self-ratings are associated with particular feelings people are experiencing.

» Frustration. We found that whenever self-ratings on their pendulums produced a result in which one side was high and the other was low, the associated feeling for both men and women was *frustration*. Frustration comes from using one side of your pendulum positively and the other side ineffectively.

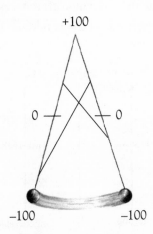

When someone is doing well on one side of the pendulum and poorly on the other, the low side drains energy. The farther apart these two points become (the more vertical the line between them), the greater the frustration the individual seems to experience.

Logically, part of what the person is doing with respect to the problem is working well; therefore, it seems like the whole thing ought to work. Often it is verbalized as "I can't figure out what I'm doing wrong. This ought to work, but it doesn't." The result is frustration.

» The Swing between Anger and Helplessness. When people's self-ratings are low on both sides of the pendulum, the associated feelings are *anger* and *helplessness*. They spend time on one side, feeling helpless that things haven't worked out and powerless to do anything about it, until they get sick and tired of the situation. Then they decide "I'm going to do something about it, dammit!" and the pendulum swings all the way to the other side. After a period of often frantic, poorly thought out, and angry efforts to resolve the problem, they become exhausted, decide "nothing will ever change," "nobody cares anyway," and give up. The pendulum swings back to the more passive side. After some time, they get fed up and explode into ineffective action once again, swinging back to the other side.

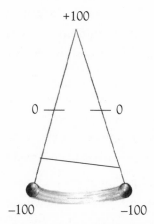

When someone is angry or helpless about a situation, they need to identify actions that will raise their self-ratings on both sides.

Conclusion

As we have suggested in earlier chapters, at high levels of performance an individual's qualities operate in paradoxical partnerships. To achieve a high performance outcome, Renee and John each needed to bring both of their paradoxical sides to bear on their problems. Further, they needed to bring the high performance expressions of their characteristics, not the extreme or nightmare expressions. Finally, they needed to take the sustained action required to get their high performance behaviors in place.

How they did this, and how you can do it with respect to your own problem situation or goal is the next step in the process.

SUMMARY OF KEY POINTS

✓ The key to high levels of performance and dealing effectively with problematic situations is to use both sides of your core paradox simultaneously in their positive expressions.

✓ The parts of this step in Paradoxical Thinking are

4a. Set up your own personal pendulum

4b. Place your goal at the top

4c. Define the expression of each side

4d. Rate your current actions with respect to your goal

✓ In high levels of performance, there is a merging of the two sides of yourself without either losing its identity, much as two melodies from two different tunes can sound wonderful together. They coexist in an intertwined relationship, which is neither a compromise nor a resolution.

✓ Fletcher's Pendulum is a tool that enables you to see which side of yourself is being expressed positively and which negatively with regard to a problem situation. You rate yourself on how positive or negative the steps are that you have already taken.

✓ Once your personal pendulum is laid out, it can be used to gain information and insights on any problem.

✓ Each side of your personal pendulum must represent a scale running from +100 through zero to –100, corresponding to your High Performance, Original, and Nightmare Oxymorons, respectively.

✓ Be sure to get the corresponding words from each oxymoron on the correct side of the pendulum, even if this means having to reverse the order of the words.

✓ It is important that the ratings on your personal pendulum be self-ratings.

✓ The most common feeling associated with self-ratings in which one side is high and the other is low is frustration. This can only be eliminated by taking action to bring up the lower side on the pendulum.

✓ The most common feelings associated with self-ratings in which both sides are low are anger and helplessness. These can only be eliminated by taking action to bring up both sides on the pendulum.

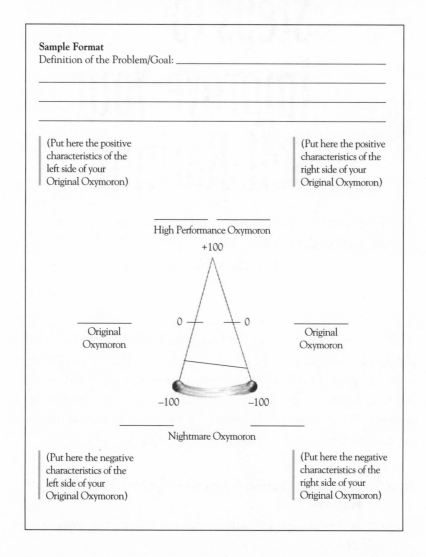

Sample Format

Definition of the Problem/Goal: _____

_____

_____

_____

(Put here the positive characteristics of the left side of your Original Oxymoron)

(Put here the positive characteristics of the right side of your Original Oxymoron)

High Performance Oxymoron

+100

0 ┼   ┼ 0

Original Oxymoron

Original Oxymoron

−100   −100

Nightmare Oxymoron

(Put here the negative characteristics of the left side of your Original Oxymoron)

(Put here the negative characteristics of the right side of your Original Oxymoron)

6

Choosing Action Steps to Improve Your Self-Ratings

There comes a moment when you have to stop revving up the car and shove it into gear.

— DAVID MAHONEY

The final step—Step 5 of the Paradoxical Thinking process—helps you develop actions you can take to raise your ratings. If you can raise both sides so that each of the paradoxical parts of yourself is being used in its most positive way, you have the makings of a high performance outcome. Since these are self-ratings, the task is to think of actions you can take that will cause you to rate yourself higher.

This step has two parts:

Step 5. Choosing Action Steps to Improve Your Self-Ratings

5a. List action steps you will take to raise your self-ratings of your lower side

5b. List action steps you will take to raise your self-ratings of your higher side

The point of this step, of course, is to take actions to improve the problem situation you are in. While in this chapter we suggest ways for you to make a list of action steps, the only reason to list action steps is to take them. Thus we write this chapter as if you are doing what you list.

If you rated yourself very low on both sides, as Renee did with respect to staying at the bank, it really doesn't make any difference which side you begin with. You need to raise your ratings on both sides significantly.

5a. List Action Steps You Will Take to Raise Your Self-Ratings of Your Lower Side

Start by doing something to raise the side you rated lower. If it can be brought up to the level of the other side, without that side dropping, your frustration will be reduced. Then the size of the pendulum swings also will be reduced, and it will be possible to concentrate more easily on raising both sides even higher, until the whole situation starts to take off in a positive direction. Then it can "go better than expected," producing a high performance result.

5b. List Action Steps You Will Take to Raise Your Self-Ratings of Your Higher Side

Once the lower side is under control and moving up, take steps to raise the higher side so the two move up in tandem.

The Renee Example

With respect to starting the flower business, Renee rated herself high on one side of her pendulum and low on the other (bold line). She was experiencing frustration. With respect to the option of staying at the bank, she rated herself negative on both sides (narrow line). She was experiencing helplessness and anger. Her pendulum was:

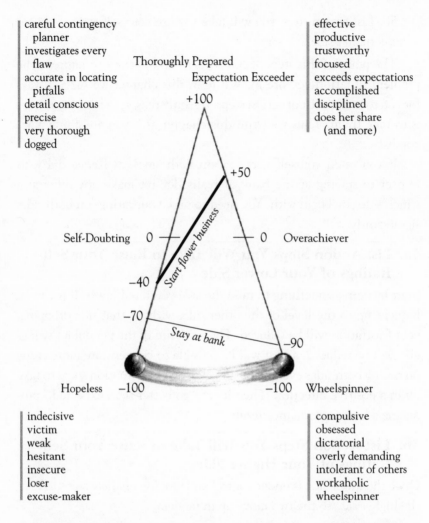

careful contingency
  planner
investigates every
  flaw
accurate in locating
  pitfalls
detail conscious
precise
very thorough
dogged

Thoroughly Prepared
Expectation Exceeder
+100

effective
productive
trustworthy
focused
exceeds expectations
accomplished
disciplined
does her share
  (and more)

+50

Self-Doubting   0

Start flower business

0   Overachiever

−40

−70

Stay at bank

−90

Hopeless   −100

−100   Wheelspinner

indecisive
victim
weak
hesitant
insecure
loser
excuse-maker

compulsive
obsessed
dictatorial
overly demanding
intolerant of others
workaholic
wheelspinner

Action Steps Renee Will Take to Raise Her Self-Ratings of Her Lower Side

How could Renee activate the more positive aspects of her self-doubting side? And how could she raise these self-ratings without diminishing the positive expression on her overachiever side? As the Fletcher's Pendulum diagram illustrates, Renee should focus on behaving more like a positive self-doubter—that is, being thorough in the exploration of what might go wrong and developing contingency plans.

Renee saw from her self-ratings that she had been too positive in her approach to starting her flower business. In an effort to be an expectation-exceeder, she had thought of lots of positive things, from her spreadsheet analysis form to strategies to counter what she saw other companies doing. *However, she hadn't taken a thorough look at what might go wrong and put contingency plans in place.* This is what she needed to do to raise her self-ratings on the thoroughly prepared side. It would also eliminate her frustration, and bring her into a positive mental state about the business venture.

Renee started by listing the actions she would take to raise her self-ratings. The first item on her list was to make an exhaustive list of all the foreseeable pitfalls if she went into the flower business. The second item was to investigate the pitfalls one-by-one and see if she could develop a way to handle each one.

When she actually created the list, it was long. She could see why she had slid into hopelessness. Then she laid out a plan to investigate each one and decide what she would do about it if it happened. Her plan included actions ranging from what she would do if sued by a client to how she would arrange a bank line of credit without significant collateral.

Renee was able to see that if she took these actions over the next few weeks, she would feel much better about going into business for herself—or—know for sure that she ought to abandon the idea. Once these actions were accomplished, she knew that if she then rated herself again, she would rate higher on the left side of her personal pendulum.

And she did. Within three weeks she developed a complete list of questions about going into business for herself, looked at the pitfalls of every alternative, made contingency plans, and developed a timetable. In other words, she began using her self-doubting tendencies in their most positive way. In fact, at the end of the three weeks, her rating on that side of Fletcher's Pendulum changed from −40 to +40, her frustration went away, and her mood swings diminished considerably.

The action steps stimulated by Renee's "self-doubting/thoroughly prepared" side also resulted in a decision that she should proceed incrementally. Instead of seeking a retail storefront to lease, she decided that she should buy a house (something she had wanted to do anyway) with a detached garage that could accommodate the modest business she already had. The business could pay a reasonable rent that would help with her mortgage, and she could move the business when she outgrew the space. A retail storefront would be some time in the future, if needed, as she already had quite a list of private clients.

Action Steps Renee Will Take to Raise Her Self-Ratings of Her Higher Side

Once Renee identified actions to raise her lower rated side, she turned to improving her higher rated side. She identified one way she could improve her self-ratings on her expectation-exceeder side. She decided to do quick yet thorough interviews of free-lancers and developed a list of people she could hire part time when large jobs required assistance.

By the time she finished her list (it took approximately three more months), she had the complete picture she needed in order to make a clear-headed decision.

An Alternative: The "Stay at the Bank" Possibility

Renee also applied her Fletcher's Pendulum with an eye to creating the conditions she needed to stay at the bank. She looked at whether she was acting as a "thoroughly prepared expectation-exceeder" with respect to her job. Was she approaching her job with the intent of exceeding expectations of herself and her boss? Was she thoroughly investigating ways to correct for the job's negatives, or was she just wallowing in helplessness and feeling anger?

She rated herself in the negative on the left side of her pendulum, as she was mired in helplessness. She also rated herself negative on the right side, as she felt she was just "doing her job" versus trying to exceed expectations.

She identified action steps she could take to raise her self-ratings. She took a number of actions to explore possibilities at her bank and also looked at two positions in other banks. However, none of them had any aesthetic component, all of them were distant emotionally, and those that paid a salary similar to her current one required a great deal of travel. As she explored, she came to the conclusion that the only type of bank that would provide what she wanted was a small town or neighborhood bank, and unfortunately her background in mergers and acquisitions was not particularly relevant.

She also realized that in a certain sense she could always go back to banking. She had a track record and a lot of expertise that would always be valuable. Running a small business was also valuable experience and would prepare her much more for the kind of lending small banks do if she ever decided to return to banking. All in all, it made sense to try the flower business. The positives of going into business for herself were much greater than anything she could foresee from staying at the bank in her current position.

The Outcome

Renee went into the flower business. She had the negatives under control. Five years later it is a thriving concern.

In the long run it is wise to apply your personal pendulum to both sides of any dilemma and to follow through with action steps to see if you can create more than one viable alternative. Then you can choose much more clearly, without wondering what might have been if you had made the other choice.

Also, there are often ways to bring the two choices together. For example, Renee might have arranged a contract with the bank to provide flowers for meeting rooms and special occasions. She didn't explore that possibility at the bank before she left, but her pendulum suggests it might have worked.

Finally, in the exploration of both sides, there are often connections between the two sides that weren't apparent before. Renee had never seen the connection between her criteria for an acceptable solution and small banks. She also hadn't seen the connection between experience with a small business operation and smaller banks. Once she did, the decision to get experience running a small business made more sense to her than it ever had.

The John Example

John's self-ratings with respect to Arthur were extremely low, as shown on the following page.

Action Steps John Will Take to Raise His Self-Ratings of His Lower Side

John looked first at his "communicator/extrovert/windbag" side and identified what he might try in his relationship with Arthur to raise his ratings.

He immediately realized that he needed to listen more to Arthur. What John needed to do was to let Arthur explain what he wanted to do and why he thought it would be better. He even thought that he

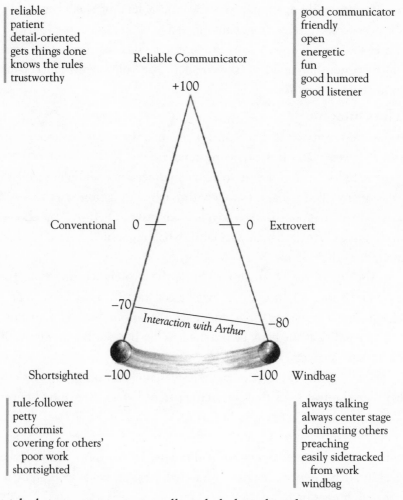

reliable
patient
detail-oriented
gets things done
knows the rules
trustworthy

good communicator
friendly
open
energetic
fun
good humored
good listener

Reliable Communicator

+100

Conventional   0

0   Extrovert

−70

Interaction with Arthur

−80

Shortsighted   −100

−100   Windbag

rule-follower
petty
conformist
covering for others'
  poor work
shortsighted

always talking
always center stage
dominating others
preaching
easily sidetracked
  from work
windbag

might bring someone in initially to help keep him from jumping onto his "preachy" platform.

He felt he would rate himself in the +50 range if he was successful at listening more to Arthur.

Action Steps John Will Take to Raise His Self-Ratings of His Higher Side

John then looked at his "reliable/conventional/shortsighted" side and asked himself how he might bring more of his "reliable" attributes into the relationship with Arthur. He identified a number of ways:

» Ask Arthur to Explain the Rules. He could go over the accounting system rules with Arthur, asking Arthur to explain why they were set up the way they were. That would get Arthur to understand the intent of the rules. Then he could ask Arthur which ones he would change if he could. Arthur could propose changes, but he would then be asked to justify them as superior in results to the rules embedded in the system as it now existed.

John felt confident that he knew accounting very well and computers well enough to bring his "detail-oriented, patient, knowledge of the rules" strengths to bear. If he were able to get detail-oriented with Arthur, thus proving his true knowledge and reliability regarding the present system, then he should be able to reestablish rapport with Arthur.

» Be Open to New Ideas. It then would be reasonable to ask that Arthur bring ideas about changes to him before implementing them.

» Think Through Changes. He could also ask Arthur questions to get him to think through all the implications—and the costs—before making changes. This would enlist Arthur's talent in a more positive way in making the accounting system more effective and more reliable.

He realized his changes in behavior toward Arthur would be awkward at first. Arthur would probably respond initially with skepticism, cynicism, and tests of his sincerity. Yet these action steps fit John well. He felt he could do them and would feel good about them because he would be expressing his "conventional/reliable" side in a much more positive way. John decided that by making these changes in the way he interacted with Arthur, he would be able to rate himself at a +50.

Taking the Actions

John made a decision to try these things immediately with Arthur. He knew they were positive steps and fit him better than the negative "checking up on Arthur" mode he had felt forced into. What he wanted was to enlist Arthur's intelligence and energy in improving things, not fight him or micromanage him.

John also felt that if he stayed centered, listened, and got Arthur to understand the intent of the rules, he would have done his part. If Arthur continued to exhibit poor judgment and cost the company dearly, John would be justified in letting him go. However, the decision would be based on giving Arthur the most room possible to make a positive contribution, not on an angry reaction to one of his mistakes.

The Outcome

The story has a wonderfully positive outcome. John's changes to express his own positive self broke the negative pattern he and Arthur were in. Arthur also was able to respond more positively. He was able to explain how much he wanted to make a contribution and to make a name for himself. He also felt that he had learned his lesson by acting before checking out the consequences. Over time Arthur and John developed a number of significant improvements in the accounting system and enhanced its utility to various regional managers. John and Arthur became an important improvement team for the whole system.

By using Fletcher's Pendulum to look at his own behavior toward Arthur, John discovered that he could use his own skills as an extrovert and a conventional "company man" to work better with Arthur. He found that once he allowed himself to be more open to Arthur's point of view, he could take better advantage of Arthur's skills.

It's Your Turn

Now try coming up with action steps for your own problem situation by working with the pendulum you created. Then imagine you have taken these actions and decide what rating you would give yourself. The idea is to find actions that if you took them, would make you rate yourself higher.

5a. List Action Steps You Will Take to Raise Your Self-Ratings of Your Lower Side

Read thoughtfully the words that are associated with the high ratings on your low side and think through actions you could take to express these positive attributes. Write at least three action steps you will take to raise your self-ratings. Brainstorm with a friend for more ideas if you have trouble coming up with some. Make your action steps relevant to the problem. If you take actions to bring up the lower side of your pendulum first, you will almost always find that you can eliminate your frustration. You will discover that things can get back on a much more positive track.

5b. List Action Steps You Will Take to Raise Your Self-Ratings of Your Higher Side

Similarly, read thoughtfully the words that are associated with high ratings on your higher side. Then write at least three action steps you will take to raise your ratings even higher. This way you will be acting even more positively in this situation. Brainstorm with a friend for more ideas if necessary. Remember to test your action steps by asking yourself whether, if you took them, you would rate yourself higher.

Work toward doing *all* the things you've listed. When you are doing, or have done, them all, see if you can identify ways to improve your self-ratings even more. The ideal is to rate yourself +100 by putting an X at the top of both scales.

Suggestions and Caveats for Choosing Action Steps

Here are a few suggestions when thinking through your action steps:

» Brainstorm with Another Person. Since identifying possible action steps is in many ways a creative exercise, it often is helpful to have someone else with whom to toss around ideas. If you are in the middle of a difficult situation, it is sometimes difficult to see what you might do differently, even with all of the help the pendulum gives. If other people help by making suggestions, *based on your pendulum*, you can assess each one. Just ask yourself whether if you took that step, you would rate yourself higher.

» Choose Actions to Raise the Lower Side of the Pendulum First. Always make sure that you define and take action *first* on your low-rated side. It is common to make the mistake of starting by picking action steps that improve the side of the pendulum on which you are already doing better. This choice will put you even further out of balance and add to your frustration. Instead, choose an action step that would cause you to rate yourself higher on the low-rated side.

» Look at Both Sides of Your Dilemma. When facing a dilemma, you will have the tendency to use your personal pendulum only with the choice (as unsatisfactory as it might be) you are most comfortable with at that moment. In the long run, it is most helpful to *apply your pendulum to both sides of any dilemma.* This way, the full range of choices will emerge, and you can ultimately make clearer, more informed decisions. It will also uncover connections between the two sides that weren't apparent.

» Beware of Dividing Your Life Between Sides of Your Oxymoron. Sometimes people discover they are unbalanced on one side of their oxymoron at work and unbalanced on the other side at home. As a result, they don't feel particularly frustrated or angry. They often believe this is a perfectly reasonable way to have organized their lives.

From our point of view it isn't. If you do this, you almost certainly are not performing fully in either place. One environment merely compensates for the other. You should work to get both sides of your oxymoron working together at work and both sides working together at home. Then there could be high performance experiences in both places.

» Strive to Have Both Sides Exist Simultaneously, without Compromise. The thousands of interviews we have done with people about their high performance experiences have clearly revealed that when people are in a high performance state, they express both sides of their paradoxical nature at more or less the same time. At high levels of performance, *there seems to be a simultaneous existence.* It is not a compromise, nor is it a resolution. People feel as if they are truly doing both at the same time.

Fortunately, virtually all people have had personal high performance experiences. When they reflect on these, they realize that the positives of both sides of their core personal paradox were present. One side didn't dominate the other. They can use these memories to understand how to deal with a problem or opportunity with the qualities of both sides fully present, and they will find that they achieve much more positive outcomes.

The same will be true for you. When you rate yourself high on both sides of the pendulum and both sides are relatively equal in force, you have moved, or are moving, into a state of high performance. Don't be satisfied with just a self-rating of, for example, +50 on both sides. This means that you are expressing both sides positively, so the frustration or anger and helplessness are minimized. However, it is not yet truly the best you can be. Work to raise your own self-ratings to +100 each. The closer to +100 each side is, the more effective you are.

» If You Rate Low on Both Sides of the Pendulum. If you rate yourself low on both sides of the pendulum, you need to accept that you are caught in a painful swing between the two sides of your contradictory nature. You will be caught in the perpetual swing between anger and helplessness until you do something radically different.

Rarely are effective decisions made when caught in this swing. Don't try to figure everything out in advance. Choose actions that will raise your self-ratings and move you into the mature expression of your contradictory nature. Then trust that much better results will follow. When you have broken the downward spiral, room will be created for anyone else who might be involved to react differently also.

SUMMARY OF KEY POINTS

✓ Once you have done your initial ratings, come up with actions you can take that will cause you to rate yourself higher.

✓ The parts of this step in Paradoxical Thinking are

5a. List action steps you will take to raise your self-ratings of your lower side

5b. List action steps you will take to raise your self-ratings of your higher side

✓ If appropriate, brainstorm about possible action steps with someone else. People who are not caught up in the problem situation are able to see possible actions that you might miss.

✓ Always act first to raise the lower-rated side. Get the two sides in balance before attempting to raise both of them toward the apex of the pendulum.

✓ Don't try too hard to "figure out" the results of your actions in advance. Assume that if you are expressing positively your core characteristics, you will be successful. Trust that the more positive results will start to appear.

✓ A change that breaks a negative cycle is always awkward at first. If another person is involved, that person will be skeptical and test your commitment to making the change. Persevere. If you are expressing both sides of your paradoxical self in a positive way, other people will change how they are interacting with you also.

✓ Work toward doing all the things on your list. Then add more. See if you can get to the point that you can rate yourself at +100 on both sides.

✓ If there are two distinct courses of action you are considering (e.g., staying at the bank or opening a floral business), apply your pendulum to both parts independently. Consider how to improve each before deciding on one of them. Often a solution that incorporates parts of both is possible.

✓ Beware of achieving "balance" in your life by being unbalanced one way at work and unbalanced the other way at home. You can't experience a high performance result in either place.

✓ Strive to keep the positives of both sides of yourself fully present. Don't compromise one for the other.

Applying Paradoxical Thinking

In order to give a sense of the broad way in which Paradoxical Thinking can be used, the next chapters provide a number of very different examples. Do not get caught in the idea that your problem has to be anything like any one of these. Get a feel for the way in which the whole process works in a variety of situations.

We have not described the entire process of creating the core paradoxes for each person, nor have we gone through every step in the Paradoxical Thinking process. Rather, we have started at the point that the Fletcher's Pendulum has been developed. Then we show how the pendulum was used to solve the problem.

A brief description of each of the examples is listed below.

» Chapter 7, "Avoiding the Loss of a Major Sale: The Case of Chris, the Overconfident Salesman"
   Chris was threatened with losing a major computer sale that he had been taking for granted. He used Paradoxical Thinking to get himself back on track.

» Chapter 8, "Resolving the Problem of a Stalled Employee in an Unexpected Way: The Case of Fred and Brad"
   This is an example of a boss-employee problem in which Paradoxical Thinking uncovered quite a different resolution than the boss expected.

» Chapter 9, "Selling a House in a Down Market: The Case of Martin, the Transferred Executive"
   This describes the problem of an executive who was transferred during the bottom of a real estate cycle. He used his pendulum to figure out how to sell his house in the difficult real estate market and still do well.

» Chapter 10, "Reestablishing Parental Communication with a Teenage Daughter: The Story of Anna and Casey"
   This describes the way a mother used her own pendulum to reestablish communication with her teenage daughter when every other tactic she and her husband had taken hadn't worked.

» Chapter 11, "Intuiting the Pendulum of Someone Else to Work Better with Them: The Case of Mike and Susan"

This chapter describes the way a subcontractor figured out what was probably the pendulum of a general manager with whom he had to work and how he used that knowledge to forge an effective working relationship.

» Chapter 12, "Using Paradoxical Thinking to Improve Team and Organization Performance"
This chapter extends the application of Paradoxical Thinking to teams and to an entire company. It describes how the executives of a small computer company that was growing rapidly used Paradoxical Thinking to create a shared vision of what paradoxical forces they were working with and how to take action to address the problems.

7

Avoiding the Loss of a Major Sale

The Case of Chris, the Overconfident Salesman

Chris was an experienced computer salesman. He had more than twenty years of selling under his belt, for three different companies. He started in the era of mainframes selling for Big Blue (IBM) and was now the head salesperson for a relatively new but stable start-up. He sold networking systems that allowed companies to have one integrated information system, connecting lots of different sizes of machines from many vendors.

Since he had worked for two of the largest and most well-known vendors, he felt he had a natural advantage in selling networks. He could talk in detail about the problems of connecting different systems, answering questions from engineers and software specialists in customer companies. He knew the weaknesses of his competitors' products and could point out ones that they tried to gloss over. He also knew how to handle problems with his company's product. Typically, when he was the lead salesperson, he won. Customers were quite confident that if they bought from him, he would help them solve their installation problems.

He had already had a good year. He personally had made his quota four months before the end of the fiscal year, and the sales force he led (twelve people) was on track for the best year ever—one that almost doubled the most optimistic forecast at the beginning of the year.

The largest potential sale that remained in his territory, one that would close before the end of his fiscal year, was a very large university-based teaching hospital. They had been in the process of converting their information systems for several years. He had sold his product to several of the hospital's departments in previous years and knew that people were happy with it. They were now in the market to purchase the backbone system that would link all of the information systems together.

Chris felt he knew Joyce, the head of information systems for the hospital, quite well. He had sold her the earlier systems and had provided input when she was thinking through the specifications for this final purchase. She called him when the specifications were ready, so he knew she was counting on a proposal from his firm. Frankly, he was expecting to make the sale.

Unfortunately, he had only recently become aware that something wasn't right. Joyce hadn't been returning his phone calls promptly, had been unavailable for a meeting that Chris had tried to set up, and told him that other vendors were bidding on the contract. Chris was suddenly very worried, and he wanted the best insight possible about how to get back on track quickly.

Chris's Core Personal Paradox

The Original Oxymoron Chris selected was "analytical cheerleader." He is a large man, six feet two inches tall or more and over two hundred pounds, and in very good physical shape. Even at his size, he runs a marathon every other year to keep himself disciplined about his physical condition. He is a very high energy, big smile, back slapping, and bear hugging person who welcomes everyone as a long lost friend. That is the side he dubbed "cheerleader." He also is very smart and analytical, with a sharp mind and an almost limitless drive to understand what the customer really needs in great detail so that he can provide it. That is the side he dubbed "analytical."

The Results of Perception-Shifting

The High Performance Oxymoron he derived from this Original Oxymoron through the process of Perception-Shifting was "people-oriented stickler-for-results." He was very pleased with this. "People-oriented" certainly described him, yet in everything he did, from his concern with customer satisfaction to the way he managed people who reported to him, results were what he was after. Woe to the person who thought his personal warmth meant he was willing to let results slide.

His Nightmare Oxymoron was "myopic ra-ra boy." When things went badly, it was usually because he was too much of a cheerleader (ra-ra) and lost his focus on the analytic details. Sometimes, however, he could also get lost in the details (myopic), getting so involved in understanding everything about the customer's business and needs that he lost sight of the bigger picture.

Setting Up His Personal Fletcher's Pendulum

In arranging his oxymorons on Fletcher's Pendulum, he found that he had to reverse both the Original Oxymoron and the Nightmare Oxymoron:

How First Written	*How Realigned for Placement on Pendulum*
HPO: People-Oriented Stickler-for-Results	People-Oriented Stickler-for-Results
OO: Analytical Cheerleader	*Cheerleader Analytical*
NO: Myopic Ra-Ra Boy	*Ra-Ra Boy Myopic*

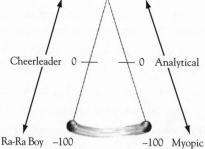

People-Oriented +100   Stickler-for-Results

Cheerleader 0 —+—   —+— 0 Analytical

Ra-Ra Boy −100   −100 Myopic

Describing How He Would Be Acting on His Cheerleader Side

Chris described how he would be acting toward Joyce and this sale if he were at each point on his "people-oriented/cheerleader/ra-ra boy" scale:

> If I were at my best, I'd be people-oriented toward this customer. I'd be really getting to know Joyce's current thinking in detail and to see the situation through her eyes. I'd be working to figure out how my product could help her succeed, in her terms.
>
> If I were in the middle, I'd be behaving like a cheerleader, telling her how excited I was about what she wanted to do and how I was sure our product would really help her. I'd be saying, "How can I help?" without really knowing her frame of reference.
>
> If I were in my nightmare toward this customer, the ra-ra boy, I'd be extolling the virtues of my product and telling her how great her ideas and suggestions were, without ever bringing the two together.

After describing himself this way, Chris then rated himself. He decided that he was above the zero point, on the "people-oriented" side of "cheerleader" with respect to Joyce and this sale. He rated himself at +30 and marked that point on his scale.

Describing How He Would Be Acting on His Analytical Side

Then Chris described the points on his "stickler-for-results/analytical/myopic" scale. He described what his behavior would be like in this way:

> If I were at my best, I'd be a real "stickler-for-results" with this customer. I'd be figuring out exactly what buying my product would do for her and selling her on the payoff. I'd be double-checking what she says she wants and suggesting lots of additional results she could get.
>
> If I were merely analytical, I'd be doing my homework with respect to my proposal, but I wouldn't be going the extra mile and suggesting things she hadn't thought of.
>
> If I were in my nightmare, I'd be myopic. I would probably be assuming there was little or no competition. I would be looking only at the hospital's request for bids, not how the competition would respond to it. I might also be lost in some of the details of the proposal, responding more to some aspect that I found particularly intriguing, whether it carried much weight in the final proposal or not.

After thinking this through, Chris decided that he was on the "myopic" side of "analytical" with respect to Joyce and this sale. He admitted that he had thought he'd get the sale so had done only superficial analyses. He rated himself at −50.

Chris's pendulum diagram looked like this:

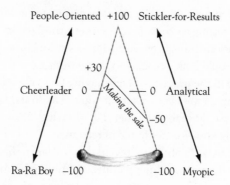

Deciding on Action Steps

Chris's honesty in rating himself, combined with the pendulum, told him immediately what was wrong. His cavalier attitude was the major part of the problem.

He wrote two action steps for himself:

1. Meet with Joyce to find out exactly what results I have to deliver to get the sale.

2. Get permission and then meet with other people in her department to see what other results I might be able to deliver. Add these to the list of results she can expect if she picks my company.

He also realized that if he met with others in her department, he could double-check her specifications. Several times he had found that he could improve on someone's specifications and win a sale that way.

The Outcome

Chris set up an appointment with Joyce that afternoon. He was on the site the next day. He spent three long days there, along with two additional technical people. At the end he was able to find a number of ways that the system he was proposing would exceed the expectations of Joyce and her department, addressing some issues they had postponed for a next generation, and doing it all for very little extra money.

When Chris's company submitted its proposal, Chris felt very good about his addressing the hospital's issues. In the meeting to submit his company's proposal and answer questions, the hospital committee found Chris had been very accurate in his depiction of what his company's system could do and how it would address the hospital's needs. He also answered a number of comparative questions between his company's system and those of his competitors.

Six weeks later, Chris's company won the bid.

Blind to the Obvious

Often people who use Fletcher's Pendulum to figure out what's wrong are surprised to find that in retrospect the answer seemed so obvious. This is true with almost any insight. As a professor in a history of science class once remarked, the classical "aha!" experience in which a person suddenly sees the answer to a question that has been a thorn in the side for a long time is widespread. However, the insight is only half of the story. The other half is that the "aha!" insight is almost universally followed by the statement, "How could I have been so stupid as to not see it?"

Why didn't Chris see what was wrong? It's hard to say. At some deep level he had gotten sloppy, confident the sale was certain, while his conscious thinking was that his bid was proceeding the way it should be. When he finally woke up to realize that his bid was in trouble, he wasn't able to think clearly and analytically. The pendulum and his self-ratings helped him admit what he had been doing wrong. From there it was a straightforward task to attempt to turn the situation around. Fortunately, he succeeded.

The virtue of Paradoxical Thinking is its simplicity. It is a powerful self-diagnostic tool that provides quick and often fresh insight into what to do differently to handle a problematic situation.

8

Resolving the Problem of a Stalled Employee in an Unexpected Way

The Case of Fred and Brad

When a manager has an employee who is not producing, and yet the employee seems competent, a reasonable tactic is to try to get the employee unblocked. Yet if the tactics that the manager chooses have the effect of draining the manager's energy, the result is a Pyrrhic victory: the employee may start producing better results, but it exacts such an emotional and physical cost on the manager that the overall impact on the work group is a drop in morale and results.

It is not easy for managers to select tactics that enhance the performance of both the manager and the employee. The following case illus-

trates how even an enlightened manager can make wrong choices in trying to improve an employee's performance, and how Paradoxical Thinking helped him sort it out.

In addition, this case illustrates how a problem can and should be
redefined in the process of trying to solve it. Initially the manager
defined the problem in an obvious way. When a solution to the problem was found, he agreed it was the solution, yet *he would not act on it.*
When he continued to complain about the problem instead of doing
something to change it, we helped him realize that there was more to
the situation than he thought. He went back to his statement of the
problem, used the pendulum to help see it in a larger context, and realized that the actual solution lay in a very different direction. Here is
the story.

The Stalled Employee

As manager of education and training for GPO Corporation, a major
office equipment manufacturer, Fred had headed a staff of twelve for
seven years. Under Fred's leadership, GPO implemented the most
promising new education and training approaches from the business
world and academia. These covered a broad range of skills and personal
development programs. Fred's training teams provided basic instruction,
personalized management coaching, and sophisticated team building
processes for thousands of employees at GPO offices across the country
and throughout the world.

Fred knew how to develop training programs for major corporate
managers and executives, but he was frustrated by one of his own
employees. Brad had been hired by Fred to produce a major conceptual
document on training that would be the foundation for future planning.
The document was intended to explain how all of the major training
programs fit together and what future directions the department should
go. But three months after Brad was hired to prepare the document,
although he had completed scores of interviews and sat in on many
meetings, the only completed pieces of the document were chapters that
Fred had drafted for Brad to use as models.

Considering a "Situational Leadership" Approach

In exasperation, Fred considered using what he called a "situational leadership" approach to resolve the problem with Brad's lack of productivity, even though he had no formal training in this method. Fred's limited understanding of situational leadership was that it was his responsibility to change his own style to improve Brad's work.

Typically, Fred's style was pretty much "hands-off." He gave his staff their responsibilities, handled the political considerations if any of his initiatives caused major ripples in the larger organization, and expected his staff to produce. Yet this style clearly wasn't working with Brad. He had reluctantly come to the conclusion that if he wanted to get effective work out of Brad, he would have to manage him tightly, direct his every move, and demand daily check-ins.

"Reluctant" accurately communicates the drained emotional energy and annoyance in Fred's voice when he talked about a change in his management style. Yet he could see no other solution. Rather than choose this distasteful alternative, he turned to Paradoxical Thinking.

Looking for a Solution with Fletcher's Pendulum

Fred's initial question was, What should he do to improve Brad's performance? He identified his Original Oxymoron, perception-shifted it, and arranged it on his personal Fletcher's Pendulum. He then rated himself on his own behavior with respect to Brad. His pendulum is shown on the facing page.

Analysis of Fred's Pendulum

Fred's Original Oxymoron was "personable controller." After Perception-Shifting, his High Performance Oxymoron became "trusting crusader." When Fred is at his best, he is leading a crusade, and he trusts his followers to produce what is needed for the crusade to be successful.

In his nightmare, Fred's controller side becomes dictator. His personable side becomes phony, what he called "phony-friendly."

From just a first look at his Fletcher's Pendulum, it was obvious to Fred that his previous approach—changing his own behavior toward tight management, directing Brad, and checking up on him—would throw Fred into his nightmare. Notice that if Fred started closely supervising and monitoring what Brad did, he would be moving *down* on the

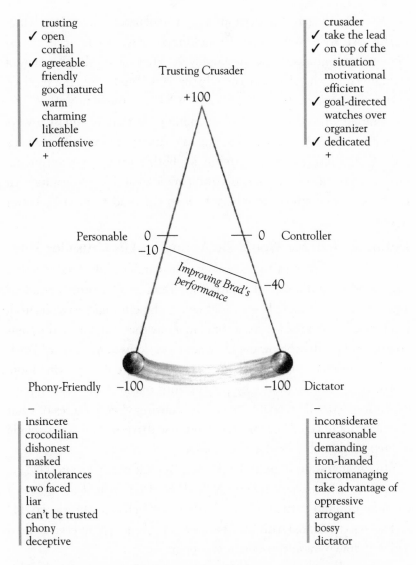

trusting
✓ open
cordial
✓ agreeable
friendly
good natured
warm
charming
likeable
✓ inoffensive
+

crusader
✓ take the lead
✓ on top of the
situation
motivational
efficient
✓ goal-directed
watches over
organizer
✓ dedicated
+

Trusting Crusader

+100

Personable   0 —|— |— 0   Controller
−10

Improving Brad's performance

−40

Phony-Friendly   −100   −100   Dictator

–
insincere
crocodilian
dishonest
masked
  intolerances
two faced
liar
can't be trusted
phony
deceptive

–
inconsiderate
unreasonable
demanding
iron-handed
micromanaging
take advantage of
oppressive
arrogant
bossy
dictator

right-hand side of his pendulum. If Fred directed Brad's every move, he would be behaving more like a dictator, micromanaging Brad in a very iron-handed way.

What positive trade-off would there be for Fred to do this? If Fred were in his nightmare space, the cost to his department, to his overall operations, and to his company would be considerable. Would it really be worthwhile to throw off a manager's performance in order to improve that of a marginal employee? Fred asked himself if that was how he wanted to approach his work life. Of course, the answer was no.

Now Fred began to understand why he had procrastinated in changing his own style. What Fred was looking for was a higher level of performance from himself *and* his employees. Fred agreed that his plan of changing his own behavior to closely supervise Brad would not produce outstanding results. The question was, What was the alternative?

The advantage of Fletcher's Pendulum is that it almost always reveals some particular way of acting in a situation that will produce a potentially high performance result for both parties. At a minimum, Fred had to positively express his own paradoxical sides in dealing with Brad. Then perhaps he could see how to get Brad to produce better results.

Defining How He Would Be Acting on His Crusader Side

Using the pendulum as an insight generator and a guide, Fred saw that he needed to find a way of approaching Brad as a "trusting crusader." Then he would be more likely to achieve high performance results from Brad. How could Fred approach Brad in a way that was personally paradoxical and positive? How could he act more "crusading" toward Brad?

Fred concluded that if he was a crusader he would be acting more motivational toward Brad, whipping up enthusiasm about Brad's report, explaining what they could do with it, drawing vivid pictures of what the department could become in the future with a powerful plan to guide it. Fred would enlist Brad in the crusade.

In order to rate himself, Fred asked himself the question, Had he been using his crusader side with Brad? Had he created a climate of expectations and enthusiasm for Brad's report? His answer was no. He had been so frustrated with Brad because of his lack of progress that Fred had withdrawn his enthusiasm and support.

He had let it be known that he was upset. His toying with the idea of becoming more dictatorial and micromanaging Brad was just the extreme expression of this feeling. He rated himself at −40 on his crusader side. It was no wonder he wasn't being very effective. He wasn't using his paradoxical qualities in their positive way. He was using phony friendliness to mask his bare tolerance of Brad's lack of production.

Defining How He Would Be Acting on His Trusting Side

Had he been trusting in his approach to Brad? What would it mean for him to be acting that way toward Brad? He decided that he would be giving Brad general directions of what to produce and then letting Brad do his job. He would simply expect an outstanding product and then get it at the right time. He went on to describe "personable" as "friendly and supportive," and described "phony-friendly" as maintaining a professional cordiality at a minimally acceptable level.

When Fred rated himself on this side of the pendulum, he claimed that he *had been* trusting of Brad. He believed that he had given Brad lots of room to prove what he could do and that Brad had essentially sat on his hands. He initially wanted to rate himself quite high.

However, we asked him to consider what he was doing now. He agreed that he had quickly lost trust in Brad when Brad didn't produce the results Fred expected. To get something to happen quickly, Fred had resorted to micromanagement. Now he was barely personable and drifting toward being phony-friendly. He rated himself at –10. He pointedly needed to remind himself that his method wasn't working and that if he resorted to being dictatorial with Brad, he was going to harm himself. It also most certainly would not produce outstanding results.

At the time, Fred was working under the premise that Brad needed to be given enough room to prove what he could do or to fail. What Brad deserved was a legitimate opportunity to prove himself or to demonstrate conclusively that he couldn't do the job, in which case Fred would be justified in taking steps to ask Brad to leave his department and find other work.

Lack of Progress

On two separate occasions, we tried to help Fred change the terms of his relationship with Brad to the more goal-directed and trusting one suggested by his Fletcher's Pendulum, without success. Fred would agree that this tactic made sense and that he ought to establish clear achievement standards that Brad's work had to meet. Then he would be able to trust Brad to show what he could do and take appropriate action if nothing was produced.

He also agreed that if Brad still did not produce an outline or a report, and if he did not show any interest in accelerating the production of the conceptual document, he ought to give Brad a written warning. Yet Fred would not change the way he was relating to Brad. Over the time of our meetings with Fred, he continued to complain about

Brad, was still periodically taking work away from him and redoing it, and continued to act angry and superficially cordial.

When Fred did not take the action steps that would move him up his own pendulum scales, even though he intellectually agreed that they were the right actions to take, we began to believe that the problem wasn't defined properly. We asked for and got permission to talk with Brad.

Looking for the Problem at a Deeper Level

Our conversations with Brad uncovered quite a different perception. Brad felt that regardless of what he produced, it was never good enough for Fred. Fred had not only given Brad feedback on his work but also angrily redone it and sent his own drafts back to Brad. In the guise of being helpful, Fred kept making it clear that he intended to do the work his way and that Brad was just supposed to "help."

In our third meeting, we asked Fred to consider whether he was truly willing to move out of the stuck pattern between him and Brad. Fred admitted that the situation was going nowhere and agreed to look deeper. We asked him to consider the possibility that the conceptual document he had asked Brad to prepare was something that he really didn't want anyone else to do. Did he feel that only he alone could do it properly?

We particularly asked him to consider the larger context. This document was intended to reflect on Fred's leadership of his department for the past seven years and to summarize the future direction of his endeavors, including directions in which to take his department. We suggested to him that in the final analysis, Fred should write the document. It had been wrong to hire Brad to do it in the first place. It wouldn't have made any difference whom he hired. He would never have allowed someone else to write it.

The Redefined Problem

To Fred's credit, he realized that we were right. His personal stake in the document was so great that he could not, in good conscience, give the task to anyone else to complete. This report about the future of his department would powerfully and directly impact the larger organization. He should handle it himself. He acknowledged that this was prob-

9

Selling a House in a Down Market

The Case of Martin, the Transferred Executive

While most of the previous examples have involved interpersonal relationships, Paradoxical Thinking is equally valuable when applied to other problems. Here is an example of how it helped a person sell his house.

The Man with Too Many Homes

Martin worked in the human resources department for the sales side of a large manufacturing corporation. A few years before our initial contact with him, Martin received a promotion, and he and his wife had returned earlier than originally expected from an assignment in Europe. Their home in upstate New York was still occupied by tenants who had signed a three-year lease, so Martin and his wife needed to find another place to live for close to a year.

With real estate prices surging, the company doing well, and his career taking off, Martin and his wife decided they would buy a second home and keep the first as a rental property. In short order, they found another house and lived in it happily for nearly two years, leasing their original house for a year at a time.

Two years after their decision to buy a second house, however, conditions changed dramatically. Martin's company downsized and decentralized substantially, and Martin was transferred to Dallas. The original house was quite rundown and dated. It still had the rust-colored carpeting and dark wallpaper decor typical of a 1970s house. The real estate boom had peaked, other companies in the region were laying off large numbers of people, and there was almost no market for houses. When the tenants' lease was up, they left, and the house was vacant.

Martin's company had a program for purchasing one home when a person was relocated, but not two. The real estate agent who had handled the original lease for them when they were in Europe offered to handle the sale of their first house. They were extremely busy with their relocation to Dallas, so they said okay, though the agent was more experienced in leasing and managing rentals. He understood that they wanted to sell, but he also suggested that he would look for tenants.

After several months on the market, there were no offers on the house and no potential tenants. Martin and his wife even thought of moving back into it to establish it as their principal residence, selling it to the company, and leasing or selling their newer home, but the prospect of moving twice, once for a very short time before relocating, was very unappealing. Yet the carrying costs were onerous. They wanted to buy a house in Dallas, but they could not even consider it with the current drain on their resources.

It was at this point of drifting, indecision, and lack of progress that Martin took our program and looked at his core paradox.

Setting Up His Personal Pendulum

When he finished selecting and Perception-Shifting his oxymorons, he created the following pendulum. His goal was to sell his original house.

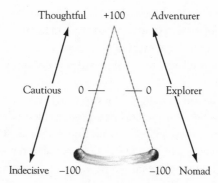

Thoughtful +100 Adventurer

Cautious 0 — 0 Explorer

Indecisive −100 −100 Nomad

Describing How He Would Be Acting on His Cautious Side

He first described how he would be acting on the "thoughtful/cautious/indecisive" side this way:

> If I were at my best, I'd be thoughtful about how I was going about selling my house. I'd be looking for clever ways of selling my house, ways that compensated for the downturn of the market.
>
> If I were in the middle, I'd be looking at different ways to sell my house, carefully evaluating them, and being very careful about downside risks. If I were considering renting, I'd be checking the contract and the references of anyone who might be interested.
>
> If I were in my nightmare, I'd be unable to make up my mind what to do. I'd find myself thinking we ought to sell at any price one day and changing my mind the next to renting it for whatever we could get while waiting for the housing market to rebound.

After describing the three points on the scale this way, Martin then rated himself. He decided that he was definitely mired in the nightmare of "indecisive." He rated himself at −70. He and his wife didn't seem to be able to make up their minds what to do. They were so busy they were just hoping something good would happen. There was nothing thoughtful or considered about their actions.

Describing How He Would Be Acting on His Explorer Side

He next described how he would be acting at each point on the "adventurer/explorer/nomad" side:

> If I were at my best, I'd be looking at this whole thing as an adventure. Moving to Dallas would be an adventure, just as moving to

Europe was. Selling my house(s) would just be part of the adventure. I'd be looking forward to trying new things and learning different ways to sell houses. I'd have a clear goal of getting the best price, but it would be important to try new things with the specific intent of learning from them.

If I were in the middle, I'd be exploring new things, but there wouldn't be the adventuresome or purposeful side to the exploration; it would be a necessary evil. I'd be finding out about whatever I had to find out about, but it would be out of a sense of having no choice.

If I were in my nightmare, I'd be nomadic, stopping on one idea for a little while, gaining a little something from it perhaps, but moving on as soon as something new attracted me or as soon as the going got rough. There would be no purposeful direction to get somewhere. It would be more reflective of wishful thinking, as in "It'll all work out somehow."

After describing these points, Martin rated himself at –50. He thought he was definitely without a sense of direction or purpose. He was going down one path, then changing direction when something seemed more attractive and going down another. Every new person with a new idea seemed able to persuade him that he should go that way.

Martin's pendulum diagram looked like this:

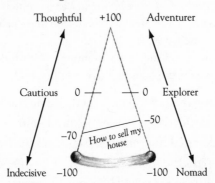

Martin's self-honesty in rating himself told him immediately what was wrong. While capable of decisive action, in this instance he was just drifting along.

Developing Action Steps

He wrote several action steps for himself:

1. He decided to fire their current real estate broker. Martin knew the agent wasn't a particularly good choice initially, but it had seemed

easier to just drift along with him. Martin resolved to set up interviews with three or four other brokers and to hire someone who
actually wanted to sell the house.

2. Martin resolved to sell the house, even if he had to take less money
   than he wanted. He was, however, willing to look at creative financing. Since his company was going to buy one of the houses, he had
   sufficient resources to carry a second mortgage.

3. Martin also decided to take much more of an adventuresome perspective on the move. Instead of reacting as if he had been "put
   upon" by the world, he decided to have his family think of various
   ways they could make the move an adventure. He decided they
   should have a goal of making the move to Dallas a high point in
   their family life.

The Outcome

Martin and his wife interviewed real estate agents and found one who
was doing well despite the downturn. She was excited by their house.

The new agent held a number of open houses. Together they
prepared a good ad for the house. Martin put the house on the internal
communication network of the company. Despite the downturn and the
downsizing, there were always people being transferred into upstate New
York.

Martin explored all sorts of creative financing. He found out what
he could offer and how to do it if his agent found a potential buyer.

A little over six weeks later, a buyer was found. The price, of course,
wasn't what it would have been a few years before, but considering the
market, Martin got a fair offer for the house. He also found that he had
learned so much about house buying and selling that when he got to
Dallas, he was in a far stronger position as a buyer than he ever had been.

The relocation went very well, and Martin and his wife are still in
Dallas four years later.

In this situation, what changed was Martin's mental attitude toward
the downsizing and the move. He adopted a positive attitude, and then
lots of other things started to fall into place. One of the effects of
Fletcher's Pendulum on people in problematic situations is that they

genuinely see a way out, a positive direction to go, so they become more positive in their attitude.

How you approach your dealings with inanimate objects is the basis of your "relationship," just as it is with another person. Your personal pendulum can help you approach such activities in a positive way.

10

Reestablishing Parental Communication with a Teenage Daughter

The Story of Anna and Casey

Anna was having difficulty with her fifteen-year-old daughter for the first time. Things seemed to be going fine with her thirteen-year-old son, but Casey was sullen, didn't follow through on her chores, and refused to clean up her room according to family agreements. She refused to participate in family discussions. Casey spent most of her time either out with friends, while promising to do her chores upon her return, or in her room reading with the door closed. The chores never got done, her room got worse daily, and her sullenness grew. She had never behaved this way before. It seemed to be more than puberty. She was, however, a top student, and her grades were not suffering.

Anna and her husband, Tom, spent many hours discussing what Casey's problem might be and how to deal with it. Anna felt she and Tom were very reasonable with their children in what they asked them to do around the house. They were expected to clear their own dishes from the table, rinse them, and put them in the dishwasher; keep their clothes and personal belongings out of the main rooms of the house; take turns emptying the garbage once a week; and clean their rooms thoroughly once a month. They also were responsible for having three dinners a week with the family. Even their children agreed that the chores and expectations were more than fair.

Casey resisted everything that was expected of her. She would not clear her dishes unless Anna and Tom demanded that she do so. Once she cleared them, she would then have to be asked to rinse them and put them in the dishwasher. She was always "going to" get around to cleaning her room the next day, but it never seemed to happen. In general, Casey was behaving morosely, acting irresponsibly, and having a detrimental effect on the entire family structure.

What Anna Had Tried

Anna and Tom tried several different tactics without any real success:

» Anna reasonably asked over and over again that Casey do her chores and clean her room. Casey did not respond.

» They tried doing more things as a family, though Casey often begged off participating with the excuse of too much homework. Casey continued to exhibit the same behavior.

» In anger, Anna twice resorted to grounding Casey until she got everything done that was expected. Both times the grounding had to be rescinded as it interfered with the honors program activities on weekends and after school that were preparing Casey for the very best universities in the country. Because both Anna and Tom worked days, they were not at home until 6:00 or 7:00 P.M. and found it difficult to force Casey to stay home to get things done.

» Anna and Tom discussed seeing a family therapist but felt that it was inappropriate to send Casey to family therapy after only a few months of this kind of behavior.

At the time we began working with Anna, she was feeling very help-less about the situation. She despaired of ever finding a proactive solu-tion. Anna used Paradoxical Thinking, as displayed on Fletcher's Pendulum, to gain a usable insight into what she might do about this problem.

Arranging Anna's Oxymorons on the Pendulum

Anna's Original Oxymoron was "gentle tiger." After Perception-Shifting, her Original Oxymoron became the High Performance Oxy-moron "loving charger" and the Nightmare Oxymoron "wimpy killer."

Anna placed her oxymorons on the pendulum and listed the corre-sponding positive and negative expressions of each side on her diagram so that she could more easily consider the range of behaviors associated with each side of the pendulum. Anna's pendulum is shown on the fol-lowing page.

Describing How She Would Be Acting on Her Gentle Side

Anna began by describing how she would be expressing her gentle side if she were doing so in the most positive, mature, and constructive way. What would she be doing if she were truly expressing her loving, gentle side in her dealings with Casey?

Anna looked at the list in the upper left and felt that she would be showing empathy toward Casey, remembering herself what it was like to be fifteen. She would be taking time to talk with Casey about what really mattered to her at this new and strange time in her life. She would be showing consideration and understanding of any difficulties Casey was having in her life. She would perhaps even be helpful to Casey, doing her chores for her (or at least with her) for a period of time to take the pressure off and just give her a break. She would be doing something that would build camaraderie between the two of them.

Anna then described how she would be expressing her gentle qual-ities in their immature, negative, and destructive mode. What kinds of things would she be doing if she was being a total wimp in this situation?

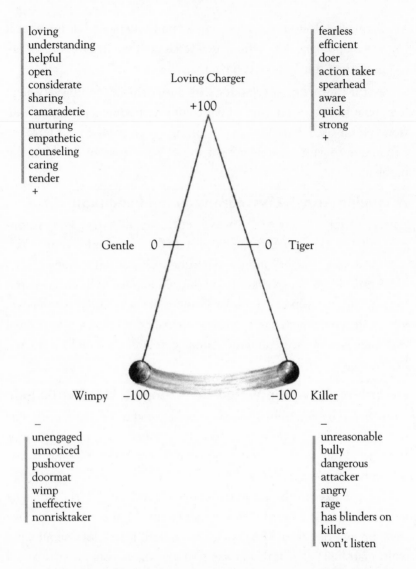

loving
understanding
helpful
open
considerate
sharing
camaraderie
nurturing
empathetic
counseling
caring
tender
+

fearless
efficient
doer
action taker
spearhead
aware
quick
strong
+

Loving Charger

+100

Gentle   0   0   Tiger

Wimpy   −100   −100   Killer

−
unengaged
unnoticed
pushover
doormat
wimp
ineffective
nonrisktaker

−
unreasonable
bully
dangerous
attacker
angry
rage
has blinders on
killer
won't listen

Anna looked at the list in the lower left and stated that she would be feeling sorry for herself. She would be feeling unheard and unnoticed by Casey. She would be totally ineffective, exemplified by Casey's not responding positively to her. She'd be a pushover, allowing Casey to walk all over her.

Describing How She Would Be Acting on Her Tiger Side

Anna then went on to describe what the mature expression of her tiger side would look like in this situation. She looked at the list of descriptors in the upper right and decided that she would be spearheading a joint activity. Anna would be directly involved with Casey. She'd be physically helping Casey clean her room and deal with some of her other chores that had piled up by doing them with her. She would be firm about her decision to do the chores together and about the time they would do them.

In describing negative behavior on her tiger side, Anna felt she would be bullying Casey to try to get her to conform. She would be yelling at her in anger, grounding her for a week at a time. She would be ignoring any signals that Casey might be sending about what was really wrong. She would refuse to even listen to Casey until she cleaned up her room and did her chores.

Rating Herself

Given that she now had a good picture of what it would look like if she were behaving both positively or negatively on each side, Anna then rated herself on each side of the pendulum.

Anna placed herself at –50 on the gentle side of the pendulum. As she described the reasons for her self-rating, she said:

> I am, in fact, being ignored and unnoticed by Casey. The result that I'm aiming for, to get Casey re-engaged with the family and family life, is not happening. I have been trying things, finding that they don't work, and then falling into feelings of despair and helplessness, which cause me to pull back and do nothing. I have been letting Casey get away with putting things off for too long and have lost credibility with Casey.

Anna placed herself at –70 on the tiger side of the pendulum. She recognized that, in fact, she had been getting very angry with Casey for her behavior. She had grounded Casey several times, felt bad about overreacting, and then relented. In refusing to listen to Casey's excuses, she was unwilling to listen at the rare times when Casey spoke to her without surliness, feeling that it was a ploy on Casey's part to get out of doing something. Anna felt she had been bullying Casey by continually reminding her how she was failing in her duties to the family, pointing out every mistake and reacting negatively to Casey's every look, word, and action.

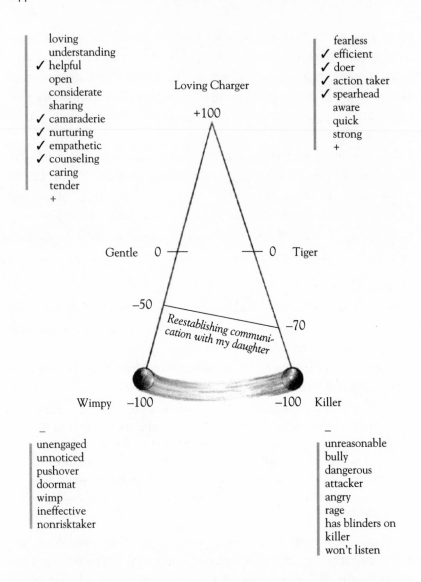

loving
understanding
✓ helpful
open
considerate
sharing
✓ camaraderie
✓ nurturing
✓ empathetic
✓ counseling
caring
tender
+

Loving Charger

+100

fearless
✓ efficient
✓ doer
✓ action taker
✓ spearhead
aware
quick
strong
+

Gentle   0   0   Tiger

−50

*Reestablishing communi-
cation with my daughter*

−70

Wimpy   −100   −100   Killer

−

unengaged
unnoticed
pushover
doormat
wimp
ineffective
nonrisktaker

−

unreasonable
bully
dangerous
attacker
angry
rage
has blinders on
killer
won't listen

Defining Specific Action Steps to Improve the Situation

Anna's first inclination had been to try to get Casey's behavior to change. However, the Paradoxical Thinking process is about Anna, not Casey. If Anna could be successful in improving and changing her behavior toward Casey—expressing her core paradoxical qualities in a positive way—her attitude and feelings about the situation would change. This change would very likely have a positive effect on Casey as well.

It is *always* initially awkward when trying to break out of a pattern of behavior that is no longer serving its original purpose. We reminded Anna that others who are used to her old behavior may initially respond by trying to force her back into the old, ineffective yet familiar, mold. However, if Anna began expressing her positive, contradictory qualities, she would most likely be successful in breaking her present ineffective interactions with Casey. Then she and her daughter could define some new ones that would better serve the situation.

Anna understood why she was so miserable once she saw that she was low on both sides of her pendulum. She was caught in the ineffective dynamic of swinging between anger and helplessness. She would go from feeling hopeless about ever resolving her relationship with Casey on the one hand to being explosively angry because she was sick and tired of Casey's irresponsible behavior. Neither reaction helped.

Since she was lower on the tiger side, at –70, she started her search for action steps to bring up that side on the pendulum. Turning to the descriptions of her mature, "tiger" self, her "charger," Anna marked the ones that called out to her immediately. She could incorporate these positive aspects of "charger" into her plan for changing her relationship with Casey.

She then proceeded to define the actions she would take:

1. Anna picked the following Saturday as the day she would help Casey to clean her room. She decided to have Tom take their son out for the entire day so that just she and Casey would be home.

2. She would insist on the date with Casey, ignoring her whines and moans about it being a bad day for her. They would do it on that day, together.

Now that she had identified two steps that applied to her tiger side (her lower rated side), she looked at her gentle side. Anna felt certain descriptors called out to her immediately, and she checkmarked them so she could incorporate these positive aspects of her loving side into her plan for changing her relationship with Casey:

3. Casey had always been a fun person to be with, and Anna wanted to make some portion of this day fun. Anna had seen an advertisement for a gourmet food delivery service that brought meals to one's home, served by waiters in full tuxedo dress. As a surprise for Casey,

Anna ordered lunch to be delivered and served to the two of them that Saturday.

Doing Something Different to Break the Cycle

These three actions gave Anna a sense of trying something different from anything she would have considered had it not been for the Perception-Shifting and Fletcher's Pendulum analysis. These actions allowed her to be helpful to Casey, and they allowed her to *do* something about the problem. By dealing with the problem together, there was a good chance to rebuild the camaraderie that had been there in the past. Anna also felt the actions allowed for the possibility of Casey opening up to her about why she was so unhappy. And finally, doing the chore with her was simply an efficient way of dealing with the real problem of cleaning up Casey's room.

The Outcome

Anna reported that her Saturday with Casey had been a very successful event. As expected, in the beginning her daughter was resentful and sullen toward Anna. Anna took over some of the more gruesome cleaning jobs and gave unemotionally charged answers to the questions that a morose Casey asked her. Within an hour and a half, Casey was asking Anna sincerely what she thought she should do about particular items. By the time lunch came, the atmosphere had already improved greatly.

Casey was delighted with the lunch surprise, and Anna knew they were on the way to better communication. As they continued the day in Casey's room, Casey began to talk more freely about her school life and her friends. It was that night, when they went to see a movie together, that Casey broke down and told her about a powerful crush she had on a schoolmate. Neither that young man nor any other showed any interest in Casey. She was heartbroken and ashamed that she was the only one of her girlfriends who'd never had a boyfriend. And Casey was sure she never would.

Once the silence was broken and deeply held secrets were brought forth, the road to communication began to be cleared. Casey soon readjusted into the family and was more easily able to confide in Anna about her problems.

In general, Paradoxical Thinking and the Fletcher's Pendulum tool have a broad range of applicability. This parent-teenager example illustrates better than any other we could pick how if you are true to your own paradoxical qualities and use them positively, other people respond well.

11

Intuiting the Pendulum of Someone Else to Work Better with Them

The Case of Mike and Susan

You may find yourself in a difficult working relationship and puzzled by how to make it better. Many times the relationship precludes actually asking the other person to go through the process of finding personal oxymorons and sharing the resulting Fletcher's Pendulum.

If you have known the person for some time, it is often possible to figure out what the other person's oxymorons and pendulum probably are. Then you can use the insights to bring out that person's positive expressions of his or her core personal paradox.

While this may come across as a somewhat manipulative use of Paradoxical Thinking and Fletcher's Pendulum, it is unfair to characterize it as such. The need for insights about how to work with another person is a nearly universal problem. We all use whatever tools and insights we can find to make working relationships more productive and satisfying. And, after all, manipulative use of any tool is possible. This is a positive example of such a use. We also comment on the payoffs and the pitfalls, the positive and negative consequences, of trying to intuit someone else's pendulum.

The Case of the Erratic General Project Manager

Mike was the president of a small, independent service firm and a subcontractor on a large project run by a much larger company. The larger company assigned as its general project manager a woman named Susan. Despite efforts to be both professional and responsible, Mike found Susan erratic. In his view, her immature behavior was destructively difficult.

From the very beginning, incident after incident supported his view. His first meeting with her had been carefully scheduled for 2:00 P.M. one afternoon at his office. He and his vice presidents were waiting for her. She didn't arrive until after 4:00 P.M., without so much as a phone call. By the time she arrived, several of his officers had left for other appointments. He had to cancel some of his other appointments to meet with her at all.

She was obviously annoyed when not everyone was there. He matter-of-factly explained that she was more than two hours late and a number of his people had been unable to stay longer. He told them to go as they had no way of knowing when she would actually arrive. He found out later, from one of her staff, that she had deliberately delayed coming and had told her staff how important it was from the very beginning to make sure subcontractors were always on their toes and willing to drop anything to serve her company. Rather than being worried about her attitude, he was angry at her immaturity.

Shortly after, he had another run-in with her about pricing. They had a signed contract that specified the prices for all of the parts. In the middle of the first significant meeting, which was meant to be a planning session, she abruptly announced that several parts of the contract would have to be renegotiated as the prices were too high. He stood his ground, indicating that it was a package deal. He could not renegotiate the prices on particular parts of the package. He had won the bid fairly based on the proposed prices. He was not willing to renegotiate. Again, she was frosty. He correctly guessed that she did not have the authority to renegotiate. This idea was her way of demonstrating to her boss what a great manager of contracts she was. If she could deliver a cost savings over what had already been negotiated, she would look particularly good. As it was, she was somewhat embarrassed in front of her own staff. Actually, two of her staff privately apologized to Mike for Susan's behavior during a break.

Continually over the next few months Susan would try some off-the-wall tactic that would catch Mike off guard, take a lot of time and energy, end up as a stand-off, and keep cooperation on the project at a minimum. Mike was tired of the energy drain. He also thought that the success of the project depended on cooperation. He could hold his own against Susan, though he couldn't be certain what damage she could do in besmirching his reputation. What he wanted was a more positive working relationship.

Over dinner one night, he and some of his staff decided to try to figure out what Susan's oxymorons and pendulum were. Based only on their experience of her behavior, they eventually created the pendulum below:

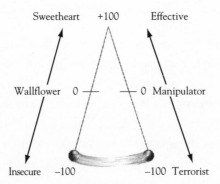

Analysis of Susan's Pendulum

The group concluded that Susan was both a rather shy person and a manipulative one. She wasn't clever enough to mask her real intentions, so it was possible to counter her negative actions, but her basically sweet, shy persona made it discomforting to realize that underneath she was willing to engage in blatant, self-serving manipulation. Thus, "wallflower manipulator" seemed a good start at characterizing her core paradox.

Mike and the group then looked at the negatives to see what they could learn. They decided that the extreme version of "wallflower" was "insecure." Similarly, they decided the extreme version of "manipulator" was "terrorist." Indeed, they all felt they had experienced her insecure side and her terrorist side. Several times when Mike had stood his ground, the situation got very ugly. Susan would simultaneously lose her professional poise and engage in threats about what she would do if Mike didn't give in. Then when she hadn't been able to follow through on her threats, she seemed to become even more insecure. Mike indeed was worried about what she was doing behind his back. He feared she was attempting to cause problems for him.

When the group turned to the positives, they saw that what she really wanted to be in her somewhat crude attempts at manipulation was "effective." She didn't have much experience running projects and didn't understand the importance of cooperation between subcontractors and the general contractor. She thought that the only way she could prove her effectiveness was to be tough with her subcontractors and to gain some advantage at their expense.

They also decided that she could be a true "sweetheart." She was naturally warm and pleasant. She also was smart and could be quite a delight to work with if only her real self could come out.

Rating Susan on "Her" Pendulum

They all rated her independently on this pendulum and then pooled their ratings. They came up with the following:

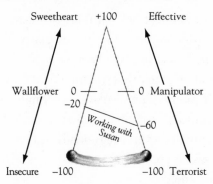

The key thing, from Mike's point of view, was to improve their working relationship, not to make Susan look bad or to push her into her nightmare space. The point was to get her to be higher on her pendulum. Then she would be more effective. The group members understood that there was no way to be certain that they really did understand what her personal paradoxes were. Susan's self-ratings also might be much higher than the group's ratings. Even so, they found this helpful as a way of collecting their experiences and ideas about how to make the relationship more productive and satisfying.

The question then became, How could they respond to Susan in a way that would move her up on her own pendulum? In effect, could they get her to be a better version of who she really was?

They came up with three ideas:

1. Never threaten her. Threats would just make her more insecure.

2. Communicate with her in an open, nonthreatening way. While this was a variation on the first idea, the notion of being "sweet" to her while gently rejecting her attempts at manipulation seemed promising. Mike felt that if he could model her best self, she would like what she saw and become more like it herself.

3. Give her opportunities to contribute in a positive way. She desperately wanted to show that she was effective. The best thing to do was to suggest ideas that Susan could champion and that she could later use as examples of her effective management. Thus the group identified several specific things they could ask that she do, all of which would be positive and helpful, and that built on her strengths.

The Outcome

The result, while not perfect, was far more satisfactory. Susan appreciated being asked to do things to help. In return, Mike and his staff thanked her and made sure her boss knew what she had done. By never reacting angrily and by patiently explaining why he couldn't do something when she threatened him, Mike slowly diminished her efforts to "terrorize" him. Eventually they managed a way of working together that was at least respectful and even occasionally fun.

The project was an outstanding success. The results were the best of any project of its kind.

Conclusions

Any tool can be used manipulatively. If a working relationship is unsatisfactory, it is reasonable to use whatever tools are available to make it better. Ideally, Susan would have learned her own oxymorons, developed her own pendulum, and used it herself. Ideally, Mike and Susan would have sat down together with their pendulums and discussed how to work together more effectively. However, it was not possible in this case, and this was the next best option.

If you believe in the overall values of this book, you will believe that when people are expressing their best selves, this allows others to do so also. Mike needed Susan to express more of her high performance self so he took steps to help her get there, even if unknown to her. These steps proved to be more effective than anything else he had tried.

12

Using Paradoxical Thinking to Improve Team and Organizational Performance

You can't solve many of today's problems by straight linear thinking. It takes leaps of faith to sense the connections that are not necessarily obvious.

— MATINA HORNER
President of Radcliffe College, 1972 to 1989

Teams, groups, departments, and often entire organizations also embody paradoxes that can be harnessed to kick performance into a much higher gear. Extending Paradoxical Thinking to situations where more than one person is involved requires that a number of the concepts be modified. The modifications are fairly straightforward. We explain them here with an example to illustrate. Also, since this chapter applies to teams, groups, departments, and entire organizations or companies, we often use only one of these terms to encompass any of the different sizes and various collections of people who work together in an organization.

A virtue of the Paradoxical Thinking tools when used in groups is the way they enhance communication and make it possible for the group to discuss conflicts, trade-offs, and even vague feelings that something is wrong that have not yet been articulated. The outcome is nearly always a greatly sharpened picture of the realities the group faces and the ways, albeit difficult, to be successful in the face of those realities.

When using Paradoxical Thinking in a group, every member is led to question assumptions the group has been making about how to be successful. Nearly always, some historical way of thinking has become ossified and taken on the form of a "sacred cow," a belief or practice regarded as above criticism or attack even though it may no longer be serving its original—or any useful—purpose. Or, without realizing it has happened, the group has fallen into general agreement on a set of assumptions. The resulting agreement about what is possible precludes exploring new avenues to improve results. The Paradoxical Thinking process breaks open these assumptions and enables the group to see the situation in a fresh way. Out of this insight come exciting new directions.

As with individuals, the first step is to have a group describe itself in terms of the paradoxical qualities of its behavior in attempting to reach its goals. Since the group hasn't been together for a lifetime, there isn't a core paradox that has the same inherently personal meaning as for individuals. However, if the group has been together *even for a short while*, we find that the members can describe their behavior as a group in terms of oxymoronic qualities.

Step 1. Finding the Group's Core Paradox

The three parts of Step 1, as applied to groups, are as follows:

1a. List the group's qualities and characteristics

1b. Combine these qualities and characteristics into paradoxical pairs using oxymorons

1c. Select one combination that describes a central conflict or tension with which the group struggles

We ask any group to start by listing words that might be used to describe it, including ones that might be used by various outside observers: corporate officers, competitors, peers in other organizations, each functional unit of the company with which the group interacts, and even the group members' secretaries. To stimulate variety we always have each individual write down his or her responses alone before sharing them with the group. Then each person explains his or her reasoning as the ideas are presented.

Some years ago we worked with a small company that we will call Paul Manufacturing (thirty managers and executives, 175 employees at the time). It dominated a niche: it had a nearly two-thirds market share for a critical component in the exploding personal computer (PC) business.

The executives had started the company themselves, led by an experienced and popular chief executive officer. While they were scrambling to meet demand, making a lot of money, and expanding quickly, they also were concerned. As a single-product company, they were vulnerable to changes in the PC business. They were also vulnerable if any of the gorillas in the broader computer world (e.g., IBM, Digital Equipment) decided to take aim at their niche.

We worked for two days with all thirty managers of the company, taking them through the five-step Paradoxical Thinking process. The managers from four different functions were present—finance, sales, manufacturing, and engineering—as well as the president, the two vice presidents, and the corporate human resources director. The group worked first in their functional units, applying the Paradoxical Thinking process to their units. They built up to applying it to Paul Manufacturing as a whole.

1a. List the Groups' Qualities and Characteristics

In their functional units, each individual made a list of the group's qualities and characteristics from a variety of points of view, presented his or her list, and explained why each word applied. The exchanges were animated. Here is how the various units described themselves.

The Finance Unit
» diligent
» incomplete: constantly playing catch-up
» hardworking
» analytical
» reactive
» often making estimates in the dark

The Manufacturing Unit
» committed
» can be trusted to come through
» miracle workers
» meet commitments
» drive
» teamwork
» doers
» unplanned
» undocumented
» flexible
» scrambling

The Sales Unit
» ambulance chasers
» pinballs ricocheting everywhere
» unfocused
» uncoordinated
» scattered
» sailors on shore leave, chasing anything in skirts
» damned good salespeople
» bringing home the bacon
» mustard cutters
» energetic

The Engineering Unit
» novices
» chain saw jugglers
» knife throwers
» knife dodgers
» knife catchers
» knife droppers
» shot-in-dark shooters
» moon promisers

We then turned to the corporation as a whole and asked the managers to consider all they had heard and formulate adjectives to describe the corporation. The list was powerful, with each person contributing either a new word or a new explanation to support one already on the list. The final set was

» opportunists
» one-eyed visionaries
» high-powered pogo sticks
» responsive
» four-stage rocket
» hard workers
» unplanned

» a stampede
» racked with growing pains
» oversexed adolescents
» multi-vectored
» novices
» ricocheting
» committed

It is difficult to convey how energized the discussion was and how many concepts were brought forth that no one had articulated before. Since each person got his or her chance to explain the words, everyone's input was listened to respectfully.

1b. Combine These Qualities and Characteristics into Paradoxical Pairs Using Oxymorons

1c. Select One Combination That Describes a Central Conflict or Tension with Which the Group Struggles

The next steps are to create paradoxical pairs and select one combination. Groups work on this by brainstorming combinations and voting on them. We keep throwing away ones with the fewest votes until only one is left. Then we double-check to see that the people really are willing to discuss the final issue honestly.

Since the Paul Manufacturing managers had not been through the individual Paradoxical Thinking process, we explained the concept of oxymorons. They proceeded to develop a list of paradoxical pairs using oxymorons and, by voting, winnow the list down to one core paradox. Here is what each group finally selected, with a brief explanation of its reasoning.

Finance Unit After much discussion the members of the finance unit selected the oxymoron

Incomplete Analysts

for themselves. Despite all their effort, their work was often late and based on incomplete and inadequate data, so it seemed to be of relatively limited utility. This was frustrating, as they were well-trained analysts who knew the importance of having powerful financial data available. They wanted to be of more value to the company as a whole. They also realized that although they had any number of analytical tools available to them as analysts, none of their training taught them how to work with incomplete data. They saw this as a major failure of their training programs.

Sales Unit After sifting through their list, the sales managers selected

Ricocheting Rockets

as their oxymoron. While they were seemingly being bounced from one objective or opportunity to another almost daily, they also were hitting their targets often enough to keep the company growing.

Manufacturing Unit The manufacturing managers settled on

Unplanned Committers

as their oxymoron. While they felt they were often having orders given to them too late, with no time to plan, they would commit to delivery dates, roll up their sleeves, and get the job done.

Engineering Unit The members of the engineering unit finally settled on

Novice Chain Saw Jugglers

as their oxymoron. They saw themselves as constantly being handed contracts for new versions of their product. They had to put them together on the run, often without the kind of testing they would have preferred. Since everyone in the PC revolution was groping in the dark to a certain extent, they all felt like novices. Nevertheless, what they put together could be dangerous to the company if it didn't work properly. It would be frightfully expensive and destroy their production schedules if they had to recall a product from the field or make large numbers of field service visits to repair something that was already shipped and didn't work. Thus, they liked the image of juggling chain saws—one slip and there would be real damage.

Paul Manufacturing as a Whole After the presentation of the oxymorons for each functional unit, each person put down his or her first choice for a combination that was both paradoxical and true of the corporation itself. As people presented their oxymorons and their reasons, the group found that they were mostly in agreement about the underlying reality, even though there were different ways it could be expressed. After much discussion, they combined a number of phrases that they felt represented them and their reality quite well:

» Multi-Vectored Four-Stage Rocket

» Responsive Stampede

» Oversexed Adolescents

» Growing-Pain-Ridden Opportunists

» Stampeding One-Eyed Visionaries

In their explanations, they all cited their feeling that they had to chase absolutely every opportunity, since with the PC field exploding, there was no way to tell which opportunities would produce the best results. Yet even with their immense commitment and energy, they felt pulled in "a thousand directions at once." They were already working six day weeks, typically twelve hours a day. They were not being smart about how they achieved their results. Ultimately they picked

Responsive Stampede

as their corporate oxymoron.

Taken together, the oxymorons of each unit, plus that of the corporation, gave quite a vibrant picture of what was going on in the company:

Finance:	Incomplete Analysts
Sales:	Ricocheting Rockets
Manufacturing:	Unplanned Committers
Engineering:	Novice Chain Saw Jugglers
Corporate:	Responsive Stampede

They had the throttle wide open and were roaring down a road that had endless twists and turns, with no brakes. They just had to pick a path—and drive!

Assessing a Culture

As consultants, the authors have been involved in various techniques of assessing the culture of a company or its readiness for change. We have also used standard questionnaire techniques for assessing morale and trying to determine the underlying problems or issues that are responsible for low morale. We have also then faced the problem of what to do to change the negatives to positives, even when the survey data were valid and reliable. We have consistently found that discussions stimulated by Paradoxical Thinking, particularly the characterizing of the departments and company in oxymorons, provide a more powerful, more dynamic, and more usable picture of what's really shaping behavior in a company than any answers to questionnaires we've seen.

Step 2. Perception-Shifting

The six parts of Step 2, as applied to groups, are as follows:

2a. List positives of preferred side

List the positive expressions of the side of the group's core paradox that it likes best.

2b. List negatives of preferred side

List the negative (extreme) expressions of the side of the group's core paradox that it likes best.

2c. List negatives of disliked side

List the negative (extreme) expressions of the side of the group's core paradox that it likes least.

2d. List positives of disliked side

List the positive expressions of the side of the group's core paradox that it likes least.

2e. Choose a High Performance Oxymoron

Choose a High Performance Oxymoron for the group that captures the positive expression of both sides of its core paradox.

2f. Choose a Nightmare Oxymoron

Choose a Nightmare Oxymoron for the group that captures the negative expression of both sides of its core paradox.

As with individuals, if a group agrees that a particular phrase is an accurate description and dislikes it, the natural reaction is to try to change it or to get depressed and become resigned to it. But often the group doesn't know what to do about it. For example, the "incomplete" part of the finance unit's "incomplete analysts" oxymoron seemed to reflect a rapidly changing reality over which they had no control. Getting rid of it—being able to do complete analyses—seemed frustratingly impossible.

With groups (as with individuals) we find that a faster route to high performance is to accept what is true and work with it. We ask individuals what is good about the part of themselves that they dislike—what is its mature and positive expression? For groups, the parallel question is, "If this is true about us, what does it mean we are good at?" We also ask individuals to identify the negatives of the parts of their behavior that they like. The parallel question for groups is, "If this is true about us, what are the negatives of this characteristic?"

Perception-Shifting is the process of expanding understanding about what each side of a paradox means. Once the meanings have been expanded or "perception-shifted," we ask group members to identify the ideal way in which they could use their paradoxical qualities (their High Performance Oxymoron) and the worst possible way their paradoxical qualities could be expressed (their Nightmare Oxymoron).

2a. List Positives of Preferred Side

The five members of the finance unit expanded on what was good about their analytic capabilities. Why was being "analysts" a good thing to them? They responded that since so many of the decisions facing the company—from pricing to inventory to cash flow projections to reducing the company's exposure to changes in the market—depended on analyses, it was critical to the company's survival that they do it well.

They listed what they saw as the positives of "analysts":

» Smart

» Grounded; solid data for their opinions

» Capable of cutting through to core truths

» Hardworking

» Detailed

» Investigative; sniff out facts in complex situations

» Able to set limits around activities

2b. List Negatives of Preferred Side

They then expanded on the negatives of their analytical capabilities. Specifically, what happens when they become too analytical, when they take "analyst" to the extreme and it begins to run them, rather than the other way around?

They rapidly saw the problems for the company if they became too analytical:

» Delay decisions; always need more time

» Never able to reach a decision; always think of more data they want to collect

» Collect every piece of data; no selectivity of the most important things to collect

» Get lost in details; no ability to see the big picture

» Averse to taking risks; always want more data for security's sake

2c. List Negatives of Disliked Side

Next they turned to the negatives of "incomplete." Specifically, we asked them to take the concept to its extreme. What would begin happening if they became even more "incomplete"?

It was easy for them to generate a list rapidly, since they did not like this side of their oxymoron:

» Recommend weak courses of action

» Opinions open to attack because the data are weak

» Analyses useless to decision makers

» Confused

» Uncertain

» Frustrated; no way to get data that are needed

» No analyses possible

2d. List Positives of Disliked Side

Finally, they made a list of the positives of "incomplete." This is always the most difficult for any individual or group to imagine—a positive manifestation of what has been seen as negative.

To help, we asked them to identify what they have probably become very good at, considering that they have had to do analytical work with incomplete data for some years. They were good analysts and knew it, so their analyses must have been valuable. What competencies had they developed as a result?

This question broke the logjam, which enabled them to formulate the following answers:

» Ability to make sense out of limited data

» See patterns and implications early

» Make inferences; see trends before others

» See ways to proactively get ahead of the competition

» Ability to be proactive

» Room for newly recognized potential

Essentially, they realized that the "incomplete" aspect of their work was only negative when seen from the perspective of an analyst. From the point of view of corporate decision makers, they had been forced to develop the skill of making sense out of limited data. Thus they could, in fact, be more valuable to the organization than they ever realized. *The group now had a new insight about their strengths that they hadn't had before.*

2e. Choose a High Performance Oxymoron

Next, they came up with a new oxymoron, one that captured the positive expression of each side. After some discussion, they selected for their High Performance Oxymoron

Pro-active Controllers

This was the image they wanted to live up to.

The high performance expression of "analysts" became "controllers." They were the financial arm of the company, so they were in fact the controllers, and controlling costs was a critical factor in the success of the company. Their analytic capability enabled them to do this task well.

The high performance expression of "incomplete" became "pro-active." Here they took the positive side of being able to work well with incomplete data and turned it into a virtue. They could help the company stay ahead of the competition and ahead of rapidly changing factors in the marketplace by interpreting scanty data well and recommending pro-active moves.

This new perception of their capabilities and what their role might be in the corporation energized the financial people dramatically. They had mainly been seen by the larger corporation as bean counters. They felt the frustration of having their analytical work be given little attention. Since the controller function is mostly saying no, they were also feeling the pressure of always seeming to undercut other people's ideas because of cost considerations.

The "pro-active" idea turned their whole attitude around. When they presented their oxymorons to the other managers and explained their reasoning, the attitudes of much of the rest of the company shifted as well.

2f. Choose a Nightmare Oxymoron

They last, and very quickly, selected as their Nightmare Oxymoron, the worst or the most ineffective expression of their paradoxical qualities. They came up with

Confused Bean Counters

At their worst, they would be going through the motions of counting lots of things, while being quite confused about what it all meant or why they were doing it. Indeed, they could remember times when they were collecting data and tabulating it furiously, yet when asked what it meant or to recommend what should be done in some difficult situation, all they could do was throw up their hands.

The Other Units

Rather than give the entire process for each of the other groups, we have listed below the high performance and the nightmare expression for each of the functions, with a brief paragraph describing the process and the insights generated.

Sales Unit

High Performance Oxymoron: Free Form Bull's-Eye-Hitters
Original Oxymoron: Ricocheting Rockets
Nightmare Oxymoron: Scattered Duds

The salespeople knew they were good. However, as the market was exploding, they were inundated with opportunities. No matter how hard they worked, they felt bounced from one opportunity to the next and torn away from one promising direction to chase another that seemed even more promising. They felt they were rocket-like in their speed of pursuit, and they hit more than their share of targets; they had a lot of freedom to be able to move from one opportunity to another.

They liked the High Performance Oxymoron of "free form bull's-eye-hitters." It meant that they could be focused in a certain direction but that there was also enough freedom for them to be smart about *how* to hit the target, maneuvering around if necessary to avoid detection by competitors. They had previously been leery of asking for more direction and focus for fear that they would have some manager second-guessing them or trying to micromanage them. "Freeform bull's-eye-hitters" was a powerful image that contained both the concept of direction-setting and focus and the concept of creativity in how they pursued their targets.

The nightmare image was truly horrifying to them—to be so scattered in so many directions at once that none of the prospects was pursued effectively, and they ended up capturing none. Nothing terrifies a salesperson more than repeatedly losing sales.

Manufacturing Unit

High Performance Oxymoron:	Flexible Results-Getters
Original Oxymoron:	Unplanned Committers
Nightmare Oxymoron:	Blindly Obedient Hesitaters

The manufacturing people felt that projects were often given to them too late, with no time to plan. They could also see that the positive expression of "unplanned" was "flexible"; not being required to follow "official" plans, they were able to adjust very quickly to whatever the customer's requirements became.

They also felt that they committed to results, regardless of whether they knew what activities were needed to get those results. They could see that the positive expression of "committers"—their willingness to make commitments and meet them—was "results-getters." While they needed to take some steps to prevent others from taking undue advantage of them, they were still rightfully proud of their capacity to respond even under the most difficult of circumstances.

The nightmare proved somewhat more difficult to envision. Eventually they saw that if the "unplanned" aspect got too extreme, the result would be confusion and a sense of being overwhelmed, which would result in a hesitation to act. They could remember times when they vacillated about taking action because they felt so dazed by the demands put on them. They described themselves in their nightmare as "hesitaters." Similarly, if their willingness to make commitments got too extreme, they could become too obedient—blindly so. They would lose perspective, and all they would be doing was agreeing to carry out whatever they were told to do. They could identify times when they had been too willing to commit to something when they should have said it was a bad idea. They chose "blindly obedient" to reflect the extreme expression of "committers."

Engineering Unit

High Performance Oxymoron: Fresh-Idea Symphony
Conductors

Original Oxymoron: Novice Chain Saw Jugglers
Nightmare Oxymoron: Showy Incompetents

The engineers saw that the positive expression of the "novice" qual-ity was a freshness, an eagerness for new ideas. At their best they could be a source of fresh ideas for the company. Similarly, the positive expres-sion of "chain saw juggling" was to be able to "orchestrate" a vast vari-ety of equipment into a smoothly running PC. They called this "'symphony conducting." At their best they were creating symphonies that were made up of fresh, exciting ideas.

The nightmare image they chose for "novice" was "incompetent," and the immature version of chain saw jugglers seemed to them obvi-ous—all show and no substance—so they chose "showy." "Showy incompetents" look good at first or from a distance but prove to be empty and untrustworthy. They could remember times when they had rushed out equipment that didn't work properly, and they couldn't fol-low up properly to integrate the new equipment into an existing system. They felt incompetent and embarrassed by their failure.

Paul Manufacturing as a Whole

High Performance Oxymoron: Multi-Engined Mass
Migration

Original Oxymoron: Responsive Stampede
Nightmare Oxymoron: Helter-Skelter Resource
Depleters

The managers all cited the feeling that they had to chase absolutely every opportunity, since there was no way to tell which ones would pro-duce the best results. Yet even with their immense commitment and energy, they were pulled in too many directions at once. They were responsive to everything, and the result was like a stampede.

They decided the positive expression of this drive toward respon-siveness would be the development of several products or product lines so that the corporation could be "multi-engined," instead of relying on the single niche they currently dominated. The positive expression of "stampede" would be a coordinated and well-synchronized "mass migration" to achieve success, everybody moving in one motion into the market. They all agreed that the nightmare, taking each side of the Original Oxymoron to an extreme, was proceeding helter-skelter at high speed and exhausting their resources.

The leadership of Paul Manufacturing now had a vivid, accurate, and paradoxical picture of how each function was currently behaving, what each function felt it would look like if performing at its best, and the nightmare pattern. The task was to get all of them to move toward their high performance image:

Finance:	Pro-Active Controllers
Sales:	Free Form Bull's-Eye-Hitters
Manufacturing:	Flexible Results-Getters
Engineering:	Fresh-Idea Symphony Conductors
Corporate:	Multi-Engined Mass Migration

The High Performance Picture

Taken together, the above descriptions provided a powerful image of where the managers and executives wanted to go with their company.

» The financial analysts would not only be controlling the flow of funds but also pro-actively helping solve a number of practical problems, such as pricing.

» Salespeople would be better focused but still would have the freedom to be flexible in order to win contracts.

» Manufacturing people would build on their flexibility to achieve results, without letting anyone take undue advantage of them.

» The engineers would be fully engaged in contributing their fresh ideas, while getting all the parts to work together seamlessly.

» The whole company would migrate en masse into the market with several product lines driving the migration.

The Nightmare Picture Likewise, the nightmares gave them a vivid image of what they wanted to move away from:

Finance:	Confused Bean Counters
Sales:	Scattered Duds
Manufacturing:	Blindly Obedient Hesitaters
Engineering:	Showy Incompetents
Corporate:	Helter-Skelter Resource-Depleters

Achieving positive movement required first rating where they currently were, and to do that they needed to define the problem situation they wanted to confront and set their goals.

Step 3. Defining the Group's Problem Situation and Setting Its Goal

The four parts of Step 3, rephrased to apply to groups, are as follows:

3a. Describe the group's unsatisfactory choices

Describe the problem situation in terms of its unsatisfactory choices, as the group currently sees them.

3b. Explain the situation's effects on the group

Explain how this problem situation affects the group itself.

3c. Assess the group's past efforts

Describe what the group has tried so far and what happened.

3d. Write a goal statement for the group with a deadline

Write a complete, measurable goal statement with a deadline.

Groups, teams and other functional units in organizations are generally more aware than are individuals of their particular missions and goals, if only because when numbers of people are involved, the missions and goals have to be written down to be communicated.

The units generally know how they are supposed to contribute to the overall success of the organization. Yet like individuals, they seem compelled often to choose between two not very appealing opposites. For example:

Reduce spending on research and development to raise profits (which may create an opening for a competitor)	or	Keep research and development high to keep products at the competitive edge (which may result in lower profits, lower stock prices, and attacks from market analysts and stockholders who want higher short-term profits)

Another way to think about dilemmas such as these is to see them as implicit "can'ts" about how the company is run: the company can't both raise research and development spending and raise profits. We start group goal-setting exercises by insisting that participants identify as many as possible of the "can'ts" embedded in either their corporate culture or their competitive environment.

A recent advertisement from Mercedes Benz provides a good illustration. This ad lists things the auto industry believes "can't be done."

You can't design cars that can be driven hard	and	expect them to last a long time
You can't build elegant cars	that also	have the lowest cost of ownership
You can't build high performance sedans	that also	lead the way in safety technology
You can't build cars that are innovative	and	dependable
You can't design cars that will look new today	and	classic tomorrow
You can't build a wide range of models	and	expect them to have high resale value

These represent, if you will, "conventional wisdom" in the auto industry about what is possible.

In the ad, the word "can't" is crossed out in each pair and replaced with the word "can." Mercedes, of course, maintains that it has solved the dilemma posed by each of these statements and has produced cars that can do both. Whether this is true or not, the nature of the thinking is what we want to highlight. Notice that each one of these claims is a pair of opposites and that what Mercedes claims it can do is achieve both sides simultaneously. Since Mercedes is one of the top two or three car companies in the world today, the Paradoxical Thinking reflected in the ad is worth noting. Each statement with the "can't" crossed out represents a genuinely high performance goal. In effect, if a car company can achieve these goals, *it will leapfrog over competitors still mired in thinking that the two sides of each statement can't be achieved together.*

Recently we worked with a client that makes a type of plastic that is elastic and can replace rubber in a number of applications. In discussing the paradoxes with which the employees routinely work, we identified one that was central to their industry's conventional wisdom: a product could either have increased structural properties (e.g., toughness, resistance to extreme temperatures) and be harder to work with and mold, or it could be easier to mold and have reduced structural properties. No one believed it was possible to do both simultaneously: to make plastic stronger and at the same time more malleable.

Yet this is the obvious "holy grail" of the industry. It ought to be the true high performance goal of the researchers—to produce a plastic that is both. By focusing on this paradoxical goal, it may be possible to review literature, design experiments, and prioritize work to make significant steps toward it, without weakening the drive to meet short-term objectives. It is obvious that if the researchers can make both improvements, the product will outdo its competition.

We use the sentence stem below and ask people to fill in the blanks:

"We can't _____ and also _____."

That is, "We can't (do something) and also (do its apparent opposite)."

Some examples are

» "We can't increase the quality of customer service and also reduce customer service costs."

» "We can't really empower our employees and also control the direction and focus of the firm."

» "We can't grow big and still preserve the 'small-family feeling' of our company."

In a group discussion, each individual has his or her own candidates for the list with which others in a group might disagree. Eventually they reach consensus on a list of implicit "can'ts."

Once people start thinking this way, they uncover many of these unconscious limitations that permeate a culture and an industry. Often conventional wisdom accumulates and doesn't get reexamined. The passage of time and the continued development of a field often makes such conventional wisdom outdated, but people rarely reexamine their assumptions.

The ability to break the limitations of conventional wisdom is critical. We know from our work with executives, for example, that it is almost always the time that they stepped out from behind the nameless shadow of what everyone else was doing and did something quite unconventional that made their careers.

When the managers and executives of Paul Manufacturing identified their own blinders, the things they felt "couldn't" be done (the generally accepted conventional wisdom of their industry about what products and strategies would work), they generated a long list; many of the ideas sparked animated discussion. Here are some of the most salient, with a brief explanation.

3a. Describe the Group's Unsatisfactory Choices

3b. Explain the Situation's Effects on the Group

Finance Unit

We can't provide the financial controls to reduce our exposure to financial risks	and also	provide optimistic forward projections of revenue to support managerial risk taking or to raise capital.

When an industry is changing so rapidly that products may become outdated almost any time, in very unpredictable ways, managers and executives have to be very quick to pick up on trends and move to take advantage of them. They need projections of potential revenue from various options. Yet in any rapidly growing company in a changing industry, financial controls and cash flow preservation are essential. Many companies fail by outrunning their revenue growth or by not controlling costs sufficiently.

The members of the finance unit felt caught between the two needs of the company. If they made optimistic projections that were incorrect, they were regarded as incompetent. If they said no to something the other executives felt was necessary for the health of the company, they were seen as shortsighted bean counters. They were frustrated by their inability to see any way out of the dilemma.

Sales Unit

We can't chase every sale	and also	provide high quality service, thus getting repeat sales from our current customers.

Since there was no real understanding at that time of the direction in which the field of computers was going to grow, it was very hard for the salespeople to be selective. They found themselves chasing every lead with seemingly equal energy and depleting their energy in the process. In particular, they found they spent less time than they would have liked handholding existing customers and developing repeat sales.

They felt themselves slowly sinking from fatigue. They felt powerless to set priorities in any way they could defend.

Manufacturing Unit

We can't turn out products as fast as we have to	and also	effectively document all the "tweakings" we do on each product to make it work.

The manufacturing people tested the assembled products and figured out what to do when something didn't work. They had become highly skilled in diagnosing glitches and "patching" systems so that they worked. However, they felt they did not have the time to document everything they did with each product. As a consequence, when a product failed in the field and needed repair, they had to try to reconstruct what, if anything, they had done to this particular machine that was unusual. On a larger scale, as products had changed and improved over the years, they did not have good records about what changes had been made for which groups of products.

They felt frustrated that there wasn't a system for documenting how each machine was assembled. However, they knew that to take the time to do that would delay the shipment of a lot of orders. It was particularly frustrating when equipment failed in the field, the field service person was called for repairs, and there was no way to help the customer.

Engineering Unit

We can't give different customers whatever they want	and still	be sure the product will work effectively when all the pieces are assembled.

Paul Manufacturing began manufacturing PC computer parts several years before when the PC industry was exploding with growth. There weren't established standards yet for many of the critical components. In order to win sales, the tendency was to promise customers whatever they wanted. However, often this meant assembling products with a huge variety of different parts. Even today there are enough incompatibilities between parts that most computers are sold as a completely assembled machine to guarantee that all the parts work together as a unit.

The promises made by salespeople who had no idea how hard it would be to produce a particular product drove the engineers crazy. Often information was lacking on many of the parts they had to bring together. As a result, far too many finished products had serious malfunctions.

Corporate

We can't focus on meeting the demand for our existing product (which is growing exponentially)	and also	diversify to become the multi-product company we need to be in order to survive.

The managers knew that Paul Manufacturing was a single-product company, raking in money as it scrambled to provide enough product for the current demand. The managers had no spare time. Yet they also knew that any product has its life cycle, and even upgrades and variations of a product have a limited life. The company needed to diversify and to have significant revenue streams from different products.

The managers felt tired and somewhat overwhelmed. They couldn't imagine how they could deliver on new products even if they did develop them.

3c. Assess the Group's Past Efforts

In working with groups, the discussion of what has been tried so far occurs during the ratings process, so it isn't necessary to do this step separately. Occasionally when a group's discussion of the ratings seems perfunctory, we do introduce it to enliven the discussion.

3d. Write a Goal Statement for the Group

Group goal setting involves the same sentence stem as with individuals:

"We're going to find a way to . . ."

To give the group a way of measuring progress toward a goal, we also have them write a "from . . . to . . ." addition to the goal statement and put a time boundary on it.

Finance Unit The finance unit chose the following goal statement:

> We're going to find a way to provide the financial controls to reduce our exposure to financial risk while providing high quality forward projections of revenue and costs related to new directions that managers feel are essential.

Next, the members of the finance unit determined what signs would tell them they were doing better and added it to their goal statement in a "from . . . to . . ." format:

Responses of our executives and managers to our work will go

- » *from* constant criticism
- » *to* active encouragement and eagerness for our input

in the next six months.

Sales Unit The sales unit developed this goal statement:

> We're going to find a way to pursue all significant new customer sales opportunities *and* get repeat sales from our current clients by doing a high quality job of serving them.

Next, the salespeople determined what signs would tell them they were moving toward their goal and added it to their goal statement in a "from . . . to . . ." format:

Our sales efforts will change

- » *from* chasing whatever customer has the closest deadline
- » *to* pursuing customers who are the top prospects according to a reasoned evaluation of each one's prospects

by the end of the next quarter.

Manufacturing Unit The manufacturing unit stated its goal this way:

> We're going to find a way to document the adaptations we've made on each product we ship while maintaining the speed at which we ship products.

Next, the manufacturing managers determined how they would know they were doing better. They wrote:

We will go

» *from* minimal and sporadic documentation of individual product variations and adaptations

» *to* effective documentation on each product that makes it repeatable and develops a "history of customer needs"

by the end of the next quarter.

Engineering Unit The engineering unit chose the following goal statement:

> We're going to find a way to provide customers with what they require while ensuring that the pieces are assembled absolutely correctly, producing a highly effective product each time.

The unit's "from . . . to . . . " statement was
We will change

» *from* often shipping products without proper testing

» *to* testing all products thoroughly before we ship them

within the next six months.

Corporate The managers developed the following goal for the corporation:

> We're going to find a way to focus on meeting the rapidly growing demand for our existing product line and simultaneously diversify into being a multi-product line company.

For their "from . . . to . . . " statement they chose
We will change

» *from* spending all our time and energy on the existing product line

» *to* spending scheduled time and energy examining possibilities of diversifying into a multi-product company

within the next nine months.

Step 4. Rating the Group on Fletcher's Pendulum

The four parts of Step 4 are as follows:

4a. Set up the group's own pendulum

4b. Place the group's goal at the top

4c. Define the expression of each side

4d. Rate the group's current actions with respect to its goal

4a. Set Up the Group's Own Pendulum

4b. Place the Group's Goal at the Top

The first two parts of this step are straightforward. Once the oxymorons are selected, they are arranged on Fletcher's Pendulum the same way as for individuals. Just remember that some of the oxymorons may need to be reversed so that each side of the pendulum represents a scale running from +100 through zero to –100. Then groups, teams, and entire organizations can rate themselves with respect to any particular goal or activity.

4c. Define the Expression of Each Side

We do not find it necessary to do this step with groups. Since the oxymorons are decided in open discussion, typically with a number of rounds of votes, the expression of each side is clear.

4d. Rate the Group's Current Actions with Respect to Its Goal

Each person does his or her own set of ratings. These are "self-ratings," but *the focus is the team or group's behavior, not just the individual's*. The question is, How would they rate their own team or group or organization on each side of the pendulum with respect to the group's goal? In developing their ratings individually, people write down their own reasons for rating the group the way they do.

The ratings are then accumulated on a large pendulum that all can see. Each individual states his or her ratings and gives an explanation and justification at the same time, usually citing examples from the group's history. Each person's individual ratings are written on the pendulum. As the ratings accumulate, and as the reasons fall into categories, a fascinating and insight-generating picture of the group takes shape before their eyes. Of most interest to the group are clusters of ratings that are quite different, where part of the group rates their behavior one way and another part of the group gives a very different set of ratings. The reasons are then explored, which results in much learning on both sides.

We believe the Paradoxical Thinking process stimulates concrete, factual communication between members of a team or group, or between different functions in an organization, that is rarely possible any other way.

Here are the ratings of the different functional groups of Paul Manufacturing and the ratings of the company as a whole. To give the reader an understanding of what generates an "average rating," we show the finance unit's individual ratings along with the average rating for each side.

Finance Unit The five finance managers arranged their oxymorons on Fletcher's Pendulum. Then they rated how well they were expressing both sides of their core paradox with respect to attaining their goal. First they marked their individual ratings on the pendulum, and then they marked the average of their individual ratings for each side. Below are their ratings with their average rating marked in bold:

> Provide the financial controls to reduce our exposure to financial risk while providing high quality forward projections of revenue and costs related to new directions that managers and executives feel are essential.

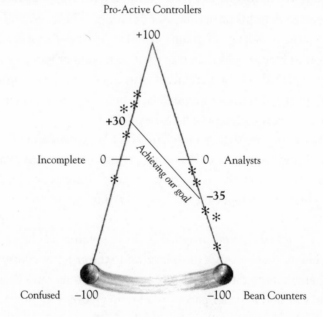

As perhaps befitted a rapidly growing entrepreneurial company, they saw themselves as doing much better in supporting managerial and executive actions than they were at the controller side of their responsibilities. The discussion as each person marked his or her ratings on the pendulum was animated (to put it mildly). There were some widely different ratings, reflecting most often the particular responsibilities of the person.

Sales Unit The salespeople arranged their oxymorons on Fletcher's Pendulum. Then they rated how well they were expressing both sides of their core paradox with respect to attaining the goal. Below are their average ratings:

> We're going to find a way to go after all significant new customer sales opportunities and get repeat sales from our current clients by doing a high quality job of serving them.

Free Form Bull's-Eye-Hitters

There were again some quite different ratings. The discussion was wide-ranging and optimistic. People listened to each other. In the end they agreed that the averages pretty well reflected reality. They were smart about how they made sales, but they were incredibly scattered. They did not have good tracking and rating systems for assessing prospects, and many good opportunities fell through the cracks while energy was expended on less promising prospects.

Manufacturing Unit The manufacturing people rated on Fletcher's Pendulum how well they were expressing both sides of their core paradox with respect to attaining their goal. Below are their average ratings:

We're going to find a way to document the adaptations we've made on each product we ship while maintaining the speed at which we ship products.

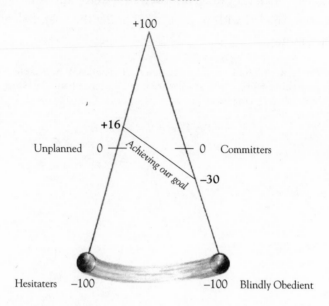

Their discussion focused on their tendency to swing back and forth, like a pendulum, when they were in the nightmare space. When they felt confused, they would swing to blind obedience to get over their confusion. This would work for awhile, but then they would not make the adjustments and modifications in products that they knew were needed. Product quality would drop, they would get blamed for it, and they would become confused again, swinging back the other way.

Their ratings indicated that they were still too blindly obedient. They needed to become more committed to getting results and take responsibility for manufacturing quality.

Engineering Unit The engineering people arranged their oxymorons on Fletcher's Pendulum. Then they rated how well they were expressing both sides of their core paradox with respect to attaining their goal. Below are their average ratings:

We're going to find a way to provide customers with what they require, while ensuring that the pieces are assembled absolutely correctly, producing a highly effective product each time.

Fresh-Idea Symphony Conductors

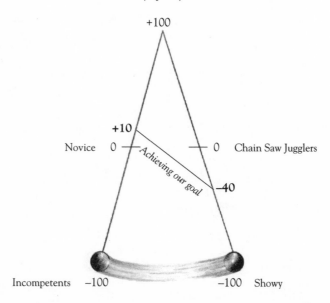

They also noticed their tendency to swing back and forth. If a product they were engineering didn't work properly, they would drop a number of features on purpose, reducing the number of variables that had to be juggled and assembled. This improved quality for awhile, but then the company's products started to fall behind the competition in their features. The engineers rushed to catch up, the features didn't mesh properly, and the group looked incompetent.

Their ratings suggested that they had good ideas about features. However, they were not effective at putting together a product that would work.

Paul Manufacturing as a Whole The corporate executives arranged their oxymorons on Fletcher's Pendulum. Then they rated how well they were expressing both sides of their core paradox with respect to attaining their goal. Below are their average ratings:

We're going to find a way to focus on meeting the rapidly growing demand for our existing product line and simultaneously diversify into being a multi-product line company.

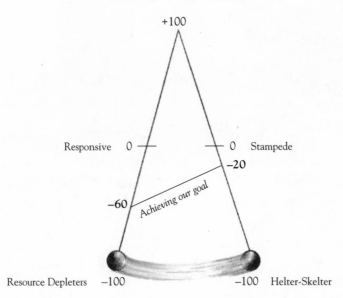

Multi-Engined Mass Migration

These composite ratings accurately reflected where Paul Manufacturing's executives and managers thought they were. They were simply rushing forward at high speed, depleting resources, and not developing new product lines. Part of the problem was they weren't being responsive at all to any other needs of their customers nor using their knowledge of these needs to guide the company's new product development. And far from producing their current product line in a carefully orchestrated, synchronized process, they were more like a stampede, running helter-skelter and bumping into each other much too often.

Paul Manufacturing and its departments were able to identify action steps to improve their self-ratings. Each department chose actions and coordinated them with the other managers so that all of their actions supported the overall corporate goal statement.

Step 5. Deciding on the Group's Action Steps

The two parts of Step 5 are as follows:

5a. List action steps the group will take to raise its self-ratings of its lower side

5b. List action steps the group will take to raise its self-ratings of its higher side

Once the ratings are done, the group members can collectively devise action steps they can take to raise their own self-ratings. The pendulum helps the people involved identify particularly effective actions they might take where before nothing seemed to work.

The theoretical framework is the same as for individuals: If the groups can simultaneously express both sides of their core paradoxes, in positive and mature ways, they will be more effective. They will have the greatest likelihood of achieving their goals.

Finance Unit

The finance people chose action steps that would improve their own self-ratings on their weaker side. They decided to concentrate on two areas of the company that had significant downside exposure (potential losses):

» Government Contracts. They needed to negotiate with the government for a higher price than they were currently getting.

» An Old Product. They and the line people felt that the industry was shifting away from one variation of their product, even though it had been earning them a lot of money. They needed to evaluate whether they should drop it and shift the resources into something else.

They decided to improve the usability of their data analyses in these two areas. By focusing on reducing exposure to potential losses, they would be using their analyst capabilities better and improve their ratings on the controller side of their oxymoron.

Sales Unit

The salespeople decided immediately to take two actions:

» Charting Opportunities. They would produce a comprehensive chart that would identify all prospects for new business, all current clients who are prospects for repeat/additional business and, even more importantly, all ways in which different clients and potential clients might have similar problems.

» Bi-Weekly Meetings. They also decided to institute comprehensive bi-weekly meetings of all salespeople to improve the coordination and focus of their efforts.

With these two steps, they felt they could get much more targeted in their work. Their ratings of themselves would go up, and they would significantly increase sales.

Manufacturing Unit

Members of the manufacturing unit decided on four different action steps:

» Documentation. They decided on a three-part documentation process: planning, assembly, and inspection. They determined ways to keep records on each part.

» Design Review. They decided on a four-part design review process: quality, reliability, producibility, and testability. They decided to require engineering to participate in the process with them before they were asked to produce a product.

» New Hiring. They decided it was time to hire a "manufacturing-engineering" person to work full time on the interface between their two units.

» Training. They decided to ask the engineers to provide them with early training on what the manufacturing unit would be building so they could get ready for the manufacturing work.

They knew these steps would cause them to rate themselves higher on the "results-getting" side of their core paradox.

Engineering Unit

The engineers quickly agreed on a number of steps to improve their ratings of themselves on their "chain saw juggler" side:

» Reduction in Variations. They decided to reduce by 10 percent the number of product variations and to immediately use that time and freed-up resources to improve their planning, coordination, and ability to engineer the systems.

» Disciplined Review. They agreed with the manufacturing unit to institute more disciplined reviews to foresee later problems with specifications, instead of committing to meeting a customer's specifications and running into problems trying to manufacture the product.

» More Testing. They decided to do more extensive testing, particularly in "at risk" contracts where the specifications were particularly difficult to meet.

» Helping Each Other. They decided to more pro-actively incorporate each other's strengths, instead of each engineer trying to put his or her stamp on each product.

They knew these steps would improve their self-ratings. They also felt the joint action with manufacturing would greatly improve throughput.

The Corporation as a Whole

The top executives decided that the action steps of the functional units would improve the efficiency of producing their current product line. They decided on one step for themselves:

» New Product Line. In the next three months they would make a decision about a new product line and commit considerable resources to it.

In this way they felt they would improve their self-ratings by improving the solidness of the company's foundation.

Paul Manufacturing continues to be a highly successful company. A few years ago it was acquired by a much larger company, but it continues under its own name, with the same leadership.

In general, the Paradoxical Thinking process can be applied by groups, teams, and entire organizations in ways that parallel those for individuals. Companies find that the improved communication and the dynamic nature of the picture that emerges is much more usable than that which results from questionnaires and other survey techniques. The groups seem to emerge already aligned about what they will do to improve results.

SUMMARY OF KEY POINTS

✓ Paradoxical Thinking is easily extended to groups of people. It involves the same five steps as for individuals, with some minor modifications.

✓ The behavior of teams, groups, departments, and organizations embodies paradoxes that can be perception-shifted in the same way a core personal paradox of an individual can be analyzed.

✓ When used by groups, Paradoxical Thinking makes it possible for groups to discuss conflicts, trade-offs, and feelings that are often difficult for people to bring up in groups and have them be heard.

✓ In Step 1, Finding the Group's Core Paradox, the group members write down their responses individually before sharing them with their group. Then each person explains the reasoning behind the ideas he or she presents.

✓ Group members discuss the most vivid paradoxical pairs and winnow the list by voting until they agree on a core paradox for the group.

✓ In Step 2, Perception-Shifting, groups need to ask, If this is true about us, what does it mean we are good at? If this is true of us, what are the weaknesses of this characteristic?

✓ Use group discussion when choosing a High Performance Oxymoron and a Nightmare Oxymoron for a group. Have group members vote, dropping the oxymorons with the fewest votes, until the list of possibilities is narrowed down to one.

✓ In Step 3, Defining the Group's Problem Situation and Setting Its Goal, skip part 3c, Assessing the Group's Past Efforts. This assessment happens naturally in the discussion.

✓ With groups, the High Performance Oxymoron becomes a powerful goal for which to strive.

✓ In understanding the paradoxical aspects of goal setting, use the sentence stem "We can't do _____ and also do _____."

✓ Use the sentence stem "We're going to find a way to . . ." to express the goal statement, incorporating the most desired result from each side of the "we can't . . . and also . . ." statement.

✓ To measure progress toward a goal, write a "from . . . to . . ." phrase for the goal statement and put a time boundary on making the change happen.

✓ In Step 4, Rating the Group on Fletcher's Pendulum, have each person individually write down where he or she thinks the group ranks. Then have each person state the rating out loud, collecting them on a master pendulum. Use an average rating for the collective picture.

✓ In Step 5, Deciding on the Group's Action Steps, the group decides on their action steps together.

✓ The discussions generated while using the Paradoxical Thinking process allow many concerns to be discussed that are difficult to bring up in any other forum.

✓ The process provides a powerful and dynamic picture of what's really shaping behavior in a company and what actions to take to improve results.

At a Glance: Paradoxical Thinking for Teams

The Steps in Paradoxical Thinking, reworded to apply to groups, are:

Step 1. Finding the Group's Core Paradox

1a. List the group's qualities and characteristics

1b. Combine these qualities and characteristics into paradoxical pairs using oxymorons

1c. Select one combination that describes a central conflict or tension with which the group struggles

Step 2. Perception-Shifting

2a. List positives of preferred side

2b. List negatives of preferred side

2c. List negatives of disliked side

2d. List positives of disliked side

2e. Choose a High Performance Oxymoron

2f. Choose a Nightmare Oxymoron

Step 3. Defining the Group's Problem Situation and Setting Its Goal

3a. Describe the group's unsatisfactory choices

3b. Explain the situation's effects on the group

3c. Assess the group's past efforts

3d. Write a goal statement for the group

Step 4. Rating the Group on Fletcher's Pendulum

4a. Set up the group's own pendulum

4b. Place the group's goal at the top

4c. Define the expression of each side

4d. Rate the group's current actions with respect to its goal

Step 5. Deciding on the Group's Action Steps

5a. List action steps the group will take to raise its self-ratings of its lower side

5b. List action steps the group will take to raise its self-ratings of its higher side

■■■

Answers and Benefits

While we have attempted to answer most of the common questions about the Paradoxical Thinking process as we explained each step, a number of more general questions are often asked that weren't easily addressed in previous chapters. These questions are more philosophical. Thus, we have created a separate chapter to address them. We hope these include your questions. Please contact us if you have one that isn't addressed.

13

Some Questions and Answers

In this chapter, we present questions that our clients commonly ask us and our answers.

1. *Do people have more than one core paradox (oxymoron)?*

We have different ideas on this one. When someone feels that he or she has two core paradoxes, Jerry tends to take this as a challenge. He will mull over the two oxymorons to see if he can come up with an underlying one that subsumes the two. Kelle tends to believe there are a few people for whom two different oxymorons are true. We both agree that in the early stages of the Paradoxical Thinking process, people think of many oxymorons that are true of them. The record is more than thirty. However, most of them turn out to be variations on a common theme. After awhile, virtually everyone seems to settle on a single underlying oxymoron (or perhaps two) that seems to capture that person's core paradox.

2. *Does a person's core paradox change over time, and thus the associated oxymoron?*

It seems to us that a person's core paradox is generally pretty stable. However, over considerable periods of time (five to ten years) we find that a number of clients report that they have changed their oxymorons.

Whether this is just normal maturation, so that a person is appropriately focused on different issues (or core tensions one must learn to manage), or whether it's some profound transformation we can't say. Our basic philosophy is that if someone reports that his or her oxymoron has changed, we accept the new one.

3. *Doesn't it make a difference what the oxymorons are of people I'm inter-acting with? If I start acting in a way that is high performance for me, won't this hurt or limit other people?*

No. It won't. All the oxymoron and pendulum tools do is enable you to bring all of yourself, fully, to whatever problematic situation or oppor-tunity you face. If you approach any other person in the situation in a way that is positive for you, you actually create room for that person to also use both sides of his or her personal paradox.

4. *What if I identify actions I should take to bring up the side I rated lower, but I really don't want to take them? I'm afraid of what might replace my familiar but ineffective pattern of swinging back and forth.*

Usually when people will not take the actions that would improve the problem situation, they have not defined the problem correctly. Somehow the apparent problem isn't truly connected to their deeper values. Once there is a clear connection—they know why they want to resolve this problem—it is much more likely they will follow through on the identified actions.

If you know what actions you "ought" to take to solve a problem and you choose not to act, at least it's your choice. You know that you have accepted the status quo and why. The actions to change the problem sit-uation are always there for you to implement if you change your mind. Perhaps you just need to wait until you are ready.

5. *If someone else knew my oxymorons and my pendulum, couldn't he or she manipulate me by forcing me into my nightmare?*

Our sense is that from the moment you really understand how to think paradoxically and understand your contradictory tendencies, it becomes very difficult for anyone else to manipulate you without your consent. You would be aware of those actions immediately. You could then decide what to do to raise your ratings of yourself. Once you took those actions, they would counter whatever the other person was doing. If you stay in your paradoxical and positive state in the face of provocation from someone else, eventually he or she has to shift. In effect, you no longer have any "hot" buttons that they can press.

6. *It seems like there are a lot of human characteristics that have no positive expressions, like "rapist" and "killer." Why do you take the position that they all have positive expressions?*

We've never seen anyone in real life who identifies "rapist" or "killer" as one of his or her core characteristics. We are not trying to dodge the question. It's just that this kind of question is more of an intellectual exercise than a real criticism of our Paradoxical Thinking process. This situation just doesn't come up in practice.

We can, as an intellectual exercise, create a pendulum for which "rapist" or "killer" are the extreme negative expressions. For example, most people agree that rape isn't so much a sexual act as a power trip. Rape is a terribly negative expression of a need to control and have power over another. The midpoint of the dimension might well be "controller" or "controlling." At its best, a need to control comes out as being very demanding about standards and quality, a "perfectionist."

However, without working with a person who truly has these characteristics and identifies them as his or her core paradox, we have no validation of our scenario. We prefer to deal with concrete examples. We've never seen one where "killer" or "rapist" was anything other than a metaphor.

7. *Since the whole process is based on self-ratings, isn't it possible to fool yourself, to put down much higher ratings than are objectively deserved?*

Yes, one can do this, but the question is, to what end? Your self-ratings help provide you with insights about some problematic situation you are trying to improve. You don't normally show your pendulum and ratings to anyone else, unless you invite someone to help you brainstorm possible solutions. No one else cares how you rate yourself, so why fake it?

In another way, the objective is to identify action steps that produce a breakthrough in some situation that currently isn't going well. If the ratings are false, chances are the insights will be similarly weak, and the actions the person takes won't successfully bring about the improvement desired. That is, the real-world situation won't respond to sloppy ratings and sloppy thinking. Paradoxical Thinking is a tool to find deeper, more powerful insights about a problematic situation, but it's not automatic and all powerful. If people want to use it incorrectly and blame the tool for their lack of insight, we can't stop them.

Finally, it is possible to show other people your pendulum and have them rate you on a problematic situation if they are familiar with it. The best way to do this is to have them rate you individually and then explain why. We use a similar collective pendulum process with groups as a team self-diagnostic device. Each person records his or her rating and explains the reasons of the rating to the group. This is a very valuable way to share perspectives and information. If all of the individual ratings are collected on a single pendulum, the resulting picture provides fascinating insight into the dynamics of the group.

8. *Isn't a lot of what you call Paradoxical Thinking just adopting a "positive mental attitude"?*

No, at least not the way that phrase is usually used. The pendulum provides real insight into the dynamics of a situation, particularly interpersonal relationships, and suggests what are usually not obvious actions to improve the situation. A positive mental attitude without powerful insights into what's wrong won't carry a person very far. Indeed, many of our clients who are initially mired in their nightmares periodically adopt positive mental attitudes about their problems. They think positively and throw themselves into resolving their problems for some time. However, if they are doing the wrong things, their situations don't change for the better and after awhile, they get discouraged. When the pendulum swings, usually one side has ratings that include a positive mental attitude about resolving the situation. But by itself, a positive mental attitude isn't enough. The actions must have a likelihood of succeeding.

9. *How does this concept of Paradoxical Thinking relate to Jung's concept of the "shadow," to polarity therapy, and to other forms of deliberately contrarian thinking, such as dialectical reasoning and, for that matter, simply playing the devil's advocate?*

The important fact to understand is that our development of this process and these tools came empirically from the analysis of high performance behaviors of people. We know that the process of Paradoxical

Thinking we have described and the tools we have explained have empirical validity. They work. Since Jung's methods, polarity therapy, and dialectical thinking also apparently have empirical validity, we imagine that they will turn out to be supportive of Paradoxical Thinking. We have not done a careful analysis of how those methods are similar to and different from Paradoxical Thinking, as we didn't derive this work from them. Paradoxical Thinking is the result of an entirely different line of thinking and analysis. We invite others to make comparisons.

10. *If I can't think of action steps to raise my ratings on the pendulum, can I get other people to help me brainstorm action steps?*

Yes, but be careful about the focus of the brainstorming. Do not ask your friend to tell you ways he or she would go about raising your ratings. Rather, brainstorm possible actions that reflect the high performance characteristics of your pendulum. Friends will have the natural tendency to revert to "If it were me, I would do such and such, so you should too." Always go back to the words and characteristics in the upper two quadrants on your pendulum diagram and use *those* to generate potential action steps.

11. *Is it possible to take groups through the Paradoxical Thinking process without having them do the process individually first?*

Yes, but we prefer not to. We spend so much time explaining the process that it is more efficient to take the members through the individual oxymoron process first. This gets them familiar with the thinking process and how the tools work. Then when we turn to the more demanding intellectual process of applying Paradoxical Thinking to groups or larger organizational units, they don't struggle with the tools. They are able to focus directly on thinking about the substantive problem.

If team members have gone through the individual process first, they usually have little difficulty coming up with an initial list of oxymorons for their team. Many times they can go directly to identifying the opposing forces affecting them, using oxymoron phrases to describe their team or unit.

12. *Why do you claim that the Paradoxical Thinking process is more valuable than other assessment techniques?*

We do not claim it is more valuable than all other assessment techniques. We do claim that it is more usable to the groups involved than most conventional assessment tools and questionnaires. Typically, assessment tools are used by a designated few, who then report the results to the people who will make decisions based on the assessment. Questionnaires rarely contribute to communication or deeper mutual understanding within a group or between groups.

Paradoxical Thinking is a tool that is "live." People use it to explore the reality of their situation and question assumptions they may have been making about how to be successful. It makes it possible for groups to discuss trade-offs and approach conflicts in a depersonalized way. As a result, everyone involved in the process can more easily see what is really shaping behavior in their company. Because of joint participation that includes individual ratings, group discussion of those ratings, and mutual understanding of the means to proceed by teams involved, the teams end up aligned around a common set of actions *and* respectful of the different perspectives that produced the creative line of action.

13. *What is the difference between the "either/or" statement used by individuals and the "can't/and also" statement used by teams, groups, and organizations?*

The difference lies only in perception. Individuals, when faced with a dilemma, often think in terms of having no more than two options, both of which they dislike. Therefore, it is couched in "I can do *either* this *or* that. The "this" and "that" are both unpleasant prospects. When faced with a dilemma, groups consider themselves to be restrained by some aspect of the dilemma that will not allow them to consider a particular approach. As a result, groups often use the term, "we *can't* do this *and also* have that occur." In this case, "this" and "that" refer to a demand and a conflicting force that seems to prevent them from meeting the demand.

14. *Do the High Performance Oxymoron and the Nightmare Oxymoron always express the same paradox found in the original core paradox?*

Yes, but not always obviously. We often find that when the original core paradox has been perception-shifted and a High Performance Oxymoron chosen, the paradoxical qualities seem to fade. They are, in fact, present but are more recognizable in the whole Perception-Shifting diagram.

On the nightmare end, when a person is expressing or acting out a Nightmare Oxymoron, the two sides are not expressed simultaneously. The person will swing from one side to the other, behaving first in one way, then swinging over to a completely different set of behaviors associated with the other side of the pendulum, and then back again. As the person is able to move his or her ratings up on each side of the pendulum scale, he or she can move more and more toward exhibiting effective paradoxical behavior.

15. *What's the relationship of High Performance Oxymorons to High Performance Patterns, the subject of your first book?*

They are closely related. High Performance Patterns are detailed descriptions of what individuals actually do when they are outstandingly successful. We can see the paradoxical qualities operating in the descriptions. When people find their core paradoxes and understand the high performance expressions, inevitably those expressions are present in their high performance stories from which their patterns were derived.

14

How to Profit from Your Contradictions

*There are pathways through . . . paradoxes if we
understand what is happening and are prepared to act
differently.*

—CHARLES HANDY
The Age of Paradox

We hope by now you have come to believe that at the center of your
being and personality you are paradoxical, for this belief has the power
to change radically how you understand and deal with contradictions
and inconsistencies in your own behavior. If you can learn to express
your contradictions positively, you can make your contradictions work
for you, and you can "profit" from them in the sense of achieving the
outcomes you want much more often in problematic situations.

It is important to make yourself fully conscious of your core paradox. Then, rather than being puzzled by contradictions and inconsistencies in your behavior, you will be able to work with them. You can
choose ways of responding to difficult situations that are much more
likely to be successful. In addition, you can recognize the phenomenon

of swinging back and forth between two negative points of view and their resulting negative actions, neither of which is effective. Becoming conscious of your core paradox allows you to recognize when this swinging is happening. That is the first step to finding a fresh line of action that has the capacity to move the situation forward.

At very high levels of performance people behave in ways that are apparently contradictory. We've cited a number of examples from the lives of famous people. We've also examined many of the descriptions in our database of how people actually achieve success. Inevitably we find that when people are most successful, they embody and express the paradoxical sides of themselves in positive and mature ways. You need to do the same to fully profit from your inherent strengths and characteristics.

Each person's core paradox is remarkably individual, probably more uniquely individual than language allows us to capture. As we have presented in the examples, virtually any characteristic has a positive, mature expression and a negative, extreme, and immature expression. High performance seems to be the result of finding the positive and mature expression of each of your core paradoxical characteristics and bringing them to bear in appropriate ways on the problem or situation that you want to improve.

Action can be a matter of deliberate choice, rather than a reaction. You can learn what your positive paradox is (what you labeled your High Performance Oxymoron), and you can "act that way" when dealing with a difficult situation. You can choose to exhibit the behavior associated with it, regardless of pressures and expectations to the contrary. Then you will start to be as effective as you can be in that difficult situation.

The Perception-Shifting step is simply a means to expand your understanding of any given characteristic so that you can find the positive expression of it. Because people often make negative judgments of some capability they have, they are blinded to its positive expressions. Too much psychological literature treats a person's core paradox as a "good side" and a "shadow." You needn't be frightened by or at the mercy of your "negative" characteristics. They are a part of you, and they are only "negative" to the degree that you don't understand how to use them constructively.

Fletcher's Pendulum is a simple self-rating instrument. However, its simplicity is what gives it its power. By rating yourself, you can easily see why you are ineffective in a situation. Once you identify and put into practice changes that would improve your ratings of yourself, the problematic situation gets better. The pendulum tool can guide you quickly to an appropriate change in behavior to become more effective in a situation.

Once you become familiar with your own Fletcher's Pendulum, you can use it as a mental guide in the middle of complex situations. If a meeting starts to go badly, for example, a quick mental rating of how well you are using the positive expression of both sides of your core paradox can give you an instant sense of how to get back on track.

We would like nothing better than that you use the tools in this book and that they work for you. If this book helps you use your paradoxical qualities consciously to make something more positive happen when faced with problem situations, we will be delighted. If this book can reduce the amount of time you spend in frustrating negative cycles, we believe you will have significantly improved your life.

We hope our insights and experience have provided a place to begin your own exploration of the art of Paradoxical Thinking.

Notes

1. Kenny Moore, "Hot Stuff," *Sports Illustrated*, 1 July 1996, 22–23.
2. Kenny Moore, "Off to a Fast Start," *Sports Illustrated*, 25 June 1984, 23.
3. Albert Rothenberg, "Creative Contradictions," *Psychology Today* June 1979, 54–62.
4. Paul Freiberger, "Bill Gates Hits the Road with IBM," *San Francisco Examiner*, 1986.
5. Sarah Mahoney, "The Ad-Ventures of Charlotte Beers," *Town & Country Monthly*, January 1993, 30.
6. Patricia Sellers, "Women, Sex and Power," *Fortune*, 5 August 1996, 42.
7. "Cocktails at Charlotte's with Martha and Darla: Businesswomen Martha Stewart, Charlotte Beers and Darla Moore," *Fortune*, 5 August 1996, 56.
8. Sam Walton with John Huey, *Sam Walton: Made in America. My Story* (New York: Bantam Books, 1993).
9. Ibid., 150.
10. Ibid., 50.
11. Ibid., 90.
12. Ibid., 151.
13. Glenn Rifkin and George Harrar, *The Ultimate Entrepreneur: The Story of Ken Olsen and Digital Equipment Corporation* (Chicago: Contemporary Books, 1988), 4–5.
14. "Book Review," *The Economist*, 25 March 1995, 93.
15. David Maraniss, *First in His Class: A Biography of Bill Clinton* (New York: Simon & Schuster, 1995), 355.
16. Richard Stengel and Robert Ajemian, "What to Make of Mario," *Time Magazine*, 2 June 1986, 28.

Annotated Bibliography

These are some of the books and articles that we have found most helpful in our thinking about Paradoxes and their relationship to high levels of human performance.

Baker, Wayne E. "The Paradox of Empowerment," *Chief Executive*. April 1994, pp. 62–65. A discussion of the paradoxes involved in empowering people in organizations. The CEO must both take control and let go.

Berne, Eric. *Games People Play: The Psychology of Human Relationships*. New York: Random House, Inc., 1964. A wonderful collection of the many kinds of repetitive, closed-loop, ultimately ineffective interaction patterns people can get trapped in, with a simple theory to understand them, and some good methods for breaking free of them.

Block, Peter. *The Empowered Manager: Positive Political Skills At Work*. San Francisco: Jossey-Bass, Inc., Publishers, 1988. Block introduced us to the pathways of "advocating our own position and yet not increasing resistance against us by our actions," as well as "the duality of self-blindness: It is easy to see political acts in others but impossible to see them in ourselves." It also breaks some of the myths people hold about power and its absoluteness.

Chawla, Sarita, and John Renesch, eds. *Learning Organizations: Developing Cultures for Tomorrow's Workplace*. Portland, Oregon: Productivity Press, 1995. Several featured chapters from individual writers that introduce core paradoxes concerning leadership. Among them: critical and timely action arising from the world of reflection; action must include not only cognitive thought but the human components of emotions, body, and spirit as well.

Collins, James C., and Jerry I. Porras. *Build to Last: Successful Habits of Visionary Companies*. New York: Harper Business, 1994. A fascinating comparison of great and near-great companies. An excellent chapter called "No Tyranny of the Or (Embrace the 'Genius of the And')" describes how the top companies refuse to choose between one or the other alternative. They manage to do both simultaneously.

Csikszentmihalyi, Mihaly. *Beyond Boredom and Anxiety*. San Francisco: Jossey-Bass, Inc., Publishers, 1977. Balancing boredom and anxiety by increasing challenges to force an increase in skill has a certain similarity to paradoxes.

Csikszentmihalyi, Mihaly. *Flow: The Psychology of Optimal Experience*. New York: Harper Perennial, 1991. Csikszentmihalyi's lifelong study of the "flow" experience has contributed immensely to what is meant by "high levels of human performance."

de Vries, Kets, and F. R. Manfred. *Organizational Paradoxes: Clinical Approaches to Management*. New York: Routledge, 1995. Kets de Vries examines leadership and power within organizations and unearths a number of associated paradoxes along the way.

Druckman, Daniel, and John A Swets. *Enhancing Human Performance: Issues, Theories, and Techniques*. Washington, D.C.: National Academy Press, 1988. A study for the Army by the National Research Council (NRC) of methods that are claimed to enhance human performance. Essentially the NRC could find no scientific data or studies to support the claims of virtually all of the methods. This is a solid "debunking" book that deflates a lot of the claims of highly promoted fads.

Druckman, Daniel, and Robert A. Bjork. *In the Mind's Eye: Enhancing Human Performance*. Washington, D.C.: National Academy Press, 1991. A second-phase, much broader report from the National Research Council of methods that are claimed to enhance human performance.

Feldman, Christina, and Jack Kornfield. *Stories of the Spirit, Stories of the Heart: Parables of the Spiritual Path from Around the World*. San Francisco: Harper Collins Publishers, 1991. A delightful and meaningful collection of parables from around the world, many of which contain inherent paradoxes within their subtle messages.

Fflew, Antony. *A Dictionary of Philosophy*. Revised Second Edition. New York: St. Martin's Press, 1984. Contains a collection of some of the most ancient paradoxes that philosophers have bantered about for centuries.

Gardner, Martin. *Aha! Gotcha: Paradoxes to Puzzle and Delight*. New York: W.H. Freeman and Company, 1982. A compendium of paradoxes in a variety of different fields.

Gilbert, Thomas F. *Human Competence: Engineering Worthy Performance*. New York: McGraw-Hill Book Company, 1978. An exceptionally original book on what human competence really is and how to achieve it in the workplace.

Handy, Charles. *The Age of Paradox*. Cambridge: Harvard Business School Press, 1994. A brilliant book about the inherent paradoxes in human actions in the world, particularly in the late twentieth century.

Harvey, Jerry B. *The Abilene Paradox and Other Meditations on Management*. New York: Lexington Books, 1988. A deeply insightful book about the subtle ways people are influenced to do things. Virtually every chapter explores a phenomenon that no one else has even noticed.

Hawken, Paul. *Growing a Business*. New York: Fireside, 1988. We've found books on entrepreneurship fascinating because they almost always involve someone taking initiative to change the way something is being done and taking a chance that his or her way will work better. The struggles individuals go through when they change the way they are interacting with someone are not that dissimilar from what happens with entrepreneurs. This is a good one of the genre.

Herman, Stanley M. *A Force of One: Reclaiming Individual Power in a Time of Teams, Work Groups and Other Crowds*. San Francisco: Jossey-Bass, Inc., Publishers, 1994. Within the pages of this book lies the concept that individuality must be maintained in order for people to be powerful collaborators and collective thinkers.

Hermanson, Dana R., and Heather M. Hermanson. "The Internal Control Paradox: What Every Manager Should Know." *Review of Business*, St. John's University, 1994. An excellent article about the paradoxes of maintaining strong internal controls and empowering people in organizations.

Hofstadter, Douglas R. *Gödel, Escher, Bach: An Eternal Golden Braid*. New York: Random House, 1980. A Pulitzer Prize winning book that explores intellectual paradox in mathematics, drawings, and music at a very deep level.

Kanter, Rosabeth Moss. *The Change Masters: Innovation for Productivity in the American Corporation*. New York: Simon & Schuster, Inc., 1983. A good chapter on the "Dilemmas of Participation" when companies are trying to bring about change.

Miller, Danny. "The Architecture of Simplicity." *Academy of Management Review*, Volume 19, Number 1, January 1993. An introduction to the Icarus Paradox in organizational terms: that which is the ultimate cause of failure has once been the source of success.

Miller, William C. *Quantum Quality: Quality Improvement through Innovation, Learning and Creativity*. New York: Quality Resources, 1993. An excellent book by one of the best in the creativity field, addressing, among many other concepts, the idea of creativity as going against what is expected.

Nisker, Wes. *Crazy Wisdom*. Berkeley: Ten Speed Press, 1990. A truly delightful little book that turns conventional wisdom on its head.

O'Neil, John R. *The Paradox of Success: When Winning at Work Means Losing at Life*. New York: Jeremy P. Tarcher/Putnam Book, 1993. Presents the dark side of public achievement and excellence. O'Neil refutes the myth that leaders who do well, are well, showing us that instead, many leaders live with personal pain and confusion, hand in hand with their excellent and highly visible public successes.

Peters, Thomas J., and Robert H. Waterman, Jr. *In Search of Excellence: Lessons from America's Best-Run Companies*. New York: Harper & Row, Publishers,

1982. The breakthrough book that actually observed what went on in well-run companies. What the authors found was often paradoxical: e.g., simultaneous loose-tight management. It is a small step to deliberately creating paradoxical behavior to manage better.

Peters, Tom. *Thriving on Chaos: Handbook for a Management Revolution.* New York: Alfred A. Knopf, 1987. The book in which Peters addresses more directly some of the paradoxes that he found.

Polanyi, Michael. *Personal Knowledge: Towards a Post-Critical Philosophy.* Chicago: University of Chicago Press, 1962. A rigorous intellectual treatment of how people come to know and accept something as true, with a particular focus on the nature of scientific knowledge.

Poole, Marshall Scott, and Andrew H. Van de Ven. "Using Paradox To Build Management And Organization Theories." *Academy of Management Review,* 1989. A theoretical discussion of different tensions or theories, the value of treating them as paradoxes, and a discussion of different ways of resolving the paradoxes.

Poundstone, William. *Labyrinths of Reason: Paradox, Puzzles, and the Frailty of Knowledge.* New York: Anchor Press, 1988. A philosophical exploration of many paradoxes and the problems of resolving them.

Quinn, Robert E., and Kim S. Cameron. *Paradox and Transformation: Toward a Theory of Change in Organization and Management.* Cambridge: Ballinger Publishing Company, 1988. A collection of articles that provide a scholarly treatment of the issues related to handling paradoxes in organizations.

Quinn, Robert E. *Beyond Rational Management: Mastering the Paradoxes and Competing Demands of High Performance.* San Francisco: Jossey-Bass, Inc., Publishers, 1988. A rich, powerful book that provides a complex theory of the different kinds of paradoxes and competing values any manager faces, and the inadequacies of rational approaches to management in accounting for how managers achieve excellence in the face of the paradoxes.

Schneider, Kirk J. *The Paradoxical Self: Toward An Understanding of Our Contradictory Nature.* New York: Plenum Publishing Corporation, 1990. A psychological and psychoanalytical discussion of various paradoxes in the human psyche, particularly dysfunctional ones.

Senge, Peter M. *The Fifth Discipline: The Art and Practice of the Learning Organization.* New York: Doubleday, 1990. A lot of the explanations of system thinking in this book expand on dilemmas and paradoxes that are found there.

Stroh, Peter, and Wynne W. Miller. "HR Professionals Should Thrive on Paradox." *Personnel Journal,* May 1993. A very good summary article of several approaches to cultivating and handling paradoxes, with particular emphasis on ones that human resources professionals confront.

Stroh, Peter, and Wynne W. Miller. "Learning to Thrive on Paradox." *Training and Development Journal*, September 1994. Similar article to the above, with more emphasis on managers handling paradoxes.

Torres, Cresencio. *The Tao of Teams: A Guide to Team Success*. San Diego: Pfeiffer & Co., 1994. An approach to leadership and group facilitation that embodies a multitude of paradoxes that are excellent cognitive and spiritual practice toward developing wise and effective leadership.

Vaill, Peter B. *Managing as a Performing Art: New Ideas for a World of Chaotic Change*. San Francisco, London: Jossey-Bass, Inc., Publishers, 1989. Addresses the "Grand Paradoxes of Management" and how to think of paradox in order to stay "friendly" with it.

Watzlawaick, Paul. *The Situation Is Hopeless, But Not Serious: The Pursuit of Unhappiness*. New York: W.W. Norton & Company, 1983. A fascinating discussion of the ways people get trapped into patterns that are not serving them at all, but they can't seem to get out of them.

Wonder, Jacquelyn, and Priscilla Donovan. *Whole-Brain Thinking: Working from Both Sides of the Brain to Achieve Peak Performance*. New York: William Morrow, 1984. Contains activities and exercises to induce using both sides of the brain simultaneously to do your best and most innovative thinking.

Appendix

We have done our best to make this book a tool you can use by yourself. We have described the steps in the Paradoxical Thinking process as clearly as we can, with detailed examples and answers to commonly asked questions. However, we also know that many people will want to go through the process with an experienced facilitator for various reasons: to introduce the ideas to a large group all at once, to facilitate team interaction about the implications of Paradoxical Thinking in their work, or simply to make sure that they do it.

For all of the above and similar reasons, the concepts introduced in *Paradoxical Thinking: How to Profit from Your Contradictions* are now offered in three separate one-day workshops:

Paradoxical Thinking for Individual Breakthroughs parallels and expands on the concepts presented in the book. Each person leaves committed to carrying out a unique and individualized action plan to achieve a goal that has previously seemed elusive. Individuals understand how to use their inherent paradoxical qualities positively in order to bring resolution to the problem or dilemma facing them.

Paradoxical Thinking for Teams, Groups, and Organizations parallels and expands on the concepts presented in Chapter 12 of the book. The Paradoxical Thinking process enable teams, groups, and whole organizations to safely explore and reshape group mindsets that have become "sacred cows"—standard and unquestioned ways of doing things that prevent innovative, dynamic thinking and limit performance. Then they learn how to use the tools of Paradoxical Thinking to promote creative group thinking and group action. The results are often a refocusing of the group's efforts in fresh and unusual ways.

Problem Solving through the Art of Paradoxical Thinking is a workshop tailored to one particular type of problem. For example, you may have become intrigued by one particular chapter: Chapter 10 on communicating with teenagers or Chapter 11 on intuiting the pendulum of someone else. Or you may want a Paradoxical Thinking workshop focused just on selling or on opening new accounts. These tailored workshops help participants apply the Paradoxical Thinking tools to a specific problem or issue, identify all points of view, and come up with creative solutions to the particular problem they face.

We also recognize that many organizations need speakers for various events, from training programs to annual meetings, from professional association gatherings to executive retreats. Paradoxical Thinking is an ideal topic for many of these, so if you have such a need, contact either Jerry or Kelle.

Presentations/Featured Speakers. As speakers, both Kelle and Jerry are dynamic, challenging, practical, and fun. People come away with their thinking expanded, with a new awareness of the ways in which they limit themselves unnecessarily, and with unique ways to conquer those limitations. Presentations are from two to four hours. Speaking engagements are typically one and a half hours or less.

Jerry Fletcher is also the author of a previous book, *Patterns of High Performance: Discovering the Ways People Work Best* (San Francisco: Berrett-Koehler, 1993). High Performance Pattern workshops are offered through High Performance Dynamics at the address below:

The High Performance Pattern Workshop takes one full day, followed by two and one-half hours of one-on-one consulting with each participant, usually in the days immediately following the workshop. The outcome is a finished High Performance Pattern for each person, which is a detailed description, written in his or her own words, of how he or she works best. Participants can then use their patterns as personal success guides to improve their results in activities of their choosing.

The High Performance Pattern Application Workshop is a four- to six-hour workshop during which participants apply their High Performance

Patterns to aspects of their current jobs that have the potential for much improvement. They develop Action Plans for improving their individual results on the job. They also learn how to apply their Patterns so that they can repeat the process. The expectation is that each person will implement the Action Plan that comes out of the workshop.

The High Performance Pattern Team-Building Workshop enables everyone on a team to learn the Pattern of everyone else. They learn how to use each other's distinct capabilities and how to support each other in being successful. They put together a Team Action Plan for achieving their objectives that enables each person to act in the way that he or she works best.

The Paradoxical Thinking workshops are the proprietary and exclusive property of High Performance Dynamics. They are currently available through:

High Performance Dynamics
56 Woodside Drive
San Anselmo, CA 94960
Tel: 415-456-5200
Fax: 415-454-1560
e-mail: HPDoffice@aol.com
e-mail: fletcher@hpdynamics.com

Kel Bergan Consulting
32 Brown Drive
Novato, CA 94947
Tel: 415-892-1464
Fax: 415-892-1464
e-mail: HPDKelle@aol.com

If you would like more information, please copy this page and mail or fax it to us.

Please contact me with information about the following:

❑ Paradoxical Thinking Workshops
❑ High Performance Pattern Workshops
❑ Bringing in Jerry Fletcher as a speaker
❑ Bringing in Kelle Olwyler as a speaker
❑ Other_____

Name: _____

Title: _____

Organization: _____

Address: _____

City: _____ State: _____ Zip: _____

Phone: _____ Fax: _____

e-mail: _____

Index

About the Authors

Jerry L. Fletcher was born and raised in a small city in Ohio. Majoring both in hard sciences (physics and mathematics) and in history, Jerry received his bachelor's degree in the history of science from Harvard. He earned his doctorate from Harvard four years later.

In the mid-seventies, as one of two senior policy analysts in education for the federal Department of Health, Education, and Welfare, Jerry began to explore every approach he could find that claimed to enable people to reach very high levels of achievement. In the process he chaired national conferences on the outer limits of human performance and became nationally recognized as an expert in the dissemination of innovations.

In 1979 Jerry left the federal government to found a company that would pursue what had become his fascination with outstanding human performance. He discovered that each person already has a process for becoming highly successful—what he called an individual's High Performance Pattern—and developed a program to help people understand and learn to use their natural processes for achieving success. The process of finding and using High Performance Patterns was described in his 1993 book, *Patterns of High Performance: Discovering the Ways People Work Best*.

More than a decade later, his company, High Performance Dynamics (HPD), has become a leader in the field of human performance and in handling the human consequences of large-scale organizational change. HPD's client list ranges from large corporations such as Shell Chemical, IBM, Digital Equipment Corporation, Procter & Gamble, and Monsanto to hundreds of smaller companies and individuals. The company's data base contains more than five thousand High Performance Patterns, the largest data base of its kind in existence.

In the course of his work, he noticed the paradoxical nature of High Performance Patterns. When people were at their best, they were often acting in ways that seemed contradictory. He remembered a parlor game he and his friends invented some years before in which they would label each other with oxymorons. They would playfully accuse each other, for example, of being an "arrogant humble-pie eater"—that is, the person was really arrogant but covered it up by acting humble and appearing to take the blame when things went wrong. Or a "dumb-acting know-it-all"—that is, the person was really a "know-it-all" but covered it by acting dumber than he was. Wonderful ribbing arguments would then ensue about whether someone's oxymoron label was true or not.

He developed a way of using oxymorons to help people become aware of their natural contradictions. He began to teach people to become comfortable with their paradoxical characteristics and to use them to achieve outstanding results, particularly in the face of seemingly irresolvable problems. His co-author, Kelle Olwyler, joined the company when the Paradoxical Thinking process was relatively new and contributed greatly to its development. This book is the outgrowth of more than ten years of experience developing and using the process with thousands of people.

Jerry lives with his wife, Kathleen, and their eleven-year-old daughter, Cassie. If you would like to talk with him to pursue any of the ideas in this book further, you can reach him c/o High Performance Dynamics, 56 Woodside Drive, San Anselmo, California 94960; 415-456-5200; Fax: 415-454-1560; e-mail addresses—HPDOffice@aol.com or fletcher@hpdynamics.com.

Kelle Olwyler was born in the United States and raised in San Miguel de Allende, Mexico. At the age of sixteen, she was sent to the United States to continue her education. Because of her bicultural upbringing, she holds a deep love for the nuances of different people and cultures. Her years of experience shuttling between Mexico and the United States, as well as traveling to Western Europe and Asia, have led her to question the accepted cultural beliefs that to be successful, people must follow prescribed rules and thinking practices. Through passionate observation she noted that throughout the world, people proved themselves to be ever varying in their manner of effectively approaching their lives.

After eight years of involvement in the business of constructing restaurants, Kelle brought her personal and business interests together when she and Jerry Fletcher met in 1986. She joined Jerry's company, High Performance Dynamics, which specializes in the technology of individual High Performance Patterns, team building, and innovative team planning processes. She became vice president after three years. She trained and managed trainers and consultants in the United States, France, and England and became the firm's senior High Performance Pattern consultant. She is an executive coach, trainer, and facilitator with extensive experience leading groups focused on reaching high levels of performance, unleashing creativity, and maximizing individual integrity and self-awareness.

In 1995, Kelle founded Kel Bergan Consulting, a training and consulting company that focuses on expanding and delivering executive coaching, innovative thinking methods, and leadership development to large and medium-sized corporations. She has also developed a branch of the firm that provides one-on-one coaching to independent consultants and small consulting firms.

She consults and trains in the United States, Latin America, and Western Europe, and has worked with Shell Oil, Unilever, Vandenberg Alimentos, Digital Equipment Corporation, Sandia National Laboratories, Pacific Gas & Electric Co., Gemini Consulting, Monsanto, Advanced Elastomer Systems, L'Institut de L'Expansion, B.F. Goodrich, The Center for Attitudinal Healing, and many others.

Kelle lives with her husband, Max Poppers, in Novato, California, and together they continue to enjoy crossing borders between the United States, Mexico, and the world. Her company's telephone and fax number is 415-892-1464. Her e-mail address is HPD Kelle@aol.com.

Berrett-Koehler Publishers

BERRETT-KOEHLER is an independent publisher of books, periodicals, and other publications at the leading edge of new thinking and innovative practice on work, business, management, leadership, stewardship, career development, human resources, entrepreneurship, and global sustainability.

Since the company's founding in 1992, we have been committed to supporting the movement toward a more enlightened world of work by publishing books, periodicals, and other publications that help us to integrate our values with our work and work lives, and to create more humane and effective organizations.

We have chosen to focus on the areas of work, business, and organizations, because these are central elements in many people's lives today. Furthermore, the work world is going through tumultuous changes, from the decline of job security to the rise of new structures for organizing people and work. We believe that change is needed at all levels— individual, organizational, community, and global—and our publications address each of these levels.

We seek to create new lenses for understanding organizations, to legitimize topics that people care deeply about but that current business orthodoxy censors or considers secondary to bottom-line concerns, and to uncover new meaning, means, and ends for our work and work lives.

See next page for other books from Berrett-Koehler Publishers

Other leading-edge business books from Berrett-Koehler Publishers

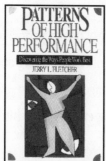

Repacking Your Bags
Lighten Your Load for the Rest of Your Life
Richard J. Leider and David A. Shapiro

LEARN HOW to climb out from under the many burdens you're carrying and find the fulfillment that's missing in your life. A simple yet elegant process teaches you to balance the demands of work, love, and place in order to create and live your own vision of success.

Paperback, 234 pages, 2/96 • ISBN 1-881052-87-7 CIP
Item no. 52877-190 $14.95

Hardcover, 1/95 • ISBN 1-881052-67-2 CIP
Item no. 52672-190 $21.95

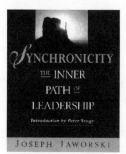

Synchronicity
The Inner Path of Leadership
Joseph Jaworski

SYNCHRONICITY is an inspirational guide to developing the most essential leadership capacity for our time: the ability to collectively shape our future. Joseph Jaworski tells the remarkable story of his journey to an understanding of the deep issues of leadership. It is a personal journey that encourages and enlightens all of us wrestling with the profound changes required in public and institutional leadership, and in our individual lives, for the 21st century.

Hardcover, 228 pages, 6/96 • ISBN 1-881052-94-X CIP
Item no. 5294X-190 $24.95

Human Resource Development Research Handbook
Linking Research and Practice
Richard A. Swanson and Elwood F. Holton III, Editors

THE HUMAN RESOURCE DEVELOPMENT RESEARCH HANDBOOK gives practitioners the tools they need to stay on the leading edge of the profession. Each chapter is written in straightforward language by a leading researcher and offers real-world examples to clearly show how research and theory are not just for academics, but are practical tools to solve everyday problems.

Paperback, 225 pages, 3/97 • ISBN 1-881052-68-0 CIP
Item no. 52680-190 $24.95

Available at your favorite bookstore, or call (800) 929-2929

Learning to Use What You Already Know

Stephen A. Stumpf and Joel R. DeLuca

Illustrated by Dan Shefelman

THIS PRACTICAL and fun-to-use guide to increasing personal and interpersonal effectiveness shows how to turn the knowledge, experience, and skills we take for granted into meaningful insights. The authors offer ways to cultivate insights—about problems, people, and situations—that bring enjoyment and build the mind's capacity to interact with people and ideas.

Hardcover, 172 pages, 8/94 • ISBN 1-881052-55-9 CIP
Item no. 52559-190 $19.95

Your Signature Path

Gaining New Perspectives on Life and Work

Geoffrey M. Bellman

YOUR SIGNATURE PATH explores the uniqueness of the mark each of us makes in the world. Bellman offers thought-provoking insights and practical tools for evaluating who you are, what you are doing, and where you want your path to lead.

Hardcover, 200 pages, 10/96 • ISBN 1-57675-004-3 CIP
Item no. 50043-190 $24.95

Artful Work

Awakening Joy, Meaning, and Commitment in the Workplace

Dick Richards

DICK RICHARDS applies the assumptions of artists about work and life to the challenges facing people and organizations in today's rapidly changing world. He reminds us that all work can be artful, and that artfulness is the key to passion and commitment. Readers will learn to take an inspired approach to their work, renewing their experience of it as a creative, participative, and purposeful endeavor.

Hardcover, 144 pages, 3/95 • ISBN 1-881052-63-X CIP
Item no. 5263X-190 $25.00

Available at your favorite bookstore, or call (800) 929-2929

BERRETT
BK
KOEHLER

I F YOU LIKE the ideas in *Paradoxical Thinking* and are interested in joining a discussion group to explore them with others, please fill out the form below and mail or fax it to:

Berrett-Koehler Publishers
450 Sansome Street, Suite 1200
San Francisco, CA 94111
Tel: (415) 288-0260
Fax: (415) 362-2512
bkpub@aol.com

Name _____

Title _____

Company _____

Address _____

_____

Tel _____

Fax _____

Email _____

Where did you buy this book?_____